46 MEN DEAD

The Royal Irish Constabulary in County Tipperary 1919–22

John Reynolds is a serving Garda Sergeant based at the Garda College in Templemore. He founded the Garda College Museum in 2002 and holds a PhD in history.

Follow John on Twitter: @johnjreynolds1

‘It is far more profitable to kill for Ireland than to die for her.’

An tÓglach, Journal of the Irish Volunteers,
15 August 1920

46 MEN DEAD

The Royal Irish Constabulary in County Tipperary 1919–22

John Reynolds

The Collins Press

First published in 2016 by
The Collins Press
West Link Park
Doughcloyne
Wilton
Cork
T12 N5EF
Ireland

A CIP record for this book is available from the British Library.

Paperback ISBN: 978-1-84889-272-9
PDF eBook ISBN: 978-1-84889-572-0
EPUB eBook ISBN: 978-1-84889-574-4
Kindle ISBN: 978-1-84889-573-7

Design and typesetting by Carrigboy Typesetting Services
Typeset in Garamond 12.5pt on 15.5pt
Printed in Malta by Gutenberg Press Limited

Contents

STATION BADGES, ROYAL IRISH CONSTABULARY.

The Station Badge which is fixed outside each Barrack of the Royal Irish Constabulary is to be painted in accordance with the above coloured diagram in future.

AUGUST, 1910.

N. CHAMBERLAIN,
Inspector-General.

(9482). Wt. 2860 - 58. 4. 500. 8/10 - Alex. Thom and Co., Ltd

The official design of the Royal Irish Constabulary Station Badge, August 1910. *(National Library of Ireland)*

Introduction: 'Omnipotent and Omniscient'[1]

> 'The Royal Irish Constabulary resembles a noble mansion of the Victorian era, still occupied but showing visible signs of decay.'[2]

Throughout the nineteenth and early twentieth centuries the Royal Irish Constabulary (RIC) performed a key role in maintaining the social order of Ireland. For almost a century, from its earliest manifestation as the Peace Preservation Force (PPF) of 1814 until complete disbandment in 1922, the RIC was intricately woven into the fabric of Irish society. In excess of 85,200 men served in various incarnations of the Irish Constabulary between 1814 and 1922.[3] Through the tragic years of the Famine (1845–52), rebellion against British rule, agrarian disputes and the gradual escalation of militant nationalism in the early twentieth century, the RIC was a pervasive and omnipresent influence in Irish society.

Anglo-Irish tensions intensified following the 1916 Rising and erupted again into open conflict in 1919. The struggle for moral authority and military supremacy between the RIC and the Irish Republican Army (IRA) became a key factor in determining the eventual outcome. During the IRA campaign of 1919 to 1922, attacks on policemen and their barracks became the primary tactic of militant nationalists, and almost 500 members of the force were killed. Apart from military operations carried out by the IRA against the police, a parallel campaign of intimidation and boycotting was directed at policemen, their families and others associated with the force such as landlords, suppliers and shopkeepers. Such measures proved effective and harked back to similar tactics used by previous generations of Irish revolutionaries. The IRA campaign against the RIC in Tipperary resulted in the deaths of forty-six policemen, the wounding of many more and the destruction, or abandonment, of dozens of barracks.

The governance of Ireland consistently tested the capabilities and patience of the most talented politicians and administrators in London. Robert Banks Jenkinson (Lord Liverpool), Tory prime minister from 1812 to 1827, described the country as 'a political phenomenon, not influenced by the same feelings as appear to affect mankind in other countries'.[4] Sir Robert Peel, elected as a Member of Parliament for Cashel in Tipperary in 1809 and the politician responsible for introducing a constabulary to Ireland, attributed the high level of disorder in the country to 'a natural predilection for outrage and a lawless life which I believe nothing can control'.[5] The perception of Ireland as having an ever-present threat of rebellion did much to ensure that the model of policing that developed in the country would always differ from that in other parts of the United Kingdom.[6] Peel was also critical of the influence of the Roman Catholic Church, stating that the prevailing religion of Ireland operated as an 'impediment rather than an aid to the ends of the civil government'.[7]

The revolutionary fervour that followed the success of the American Revolution in 1776 and the French Revolution in 1789 inspired a new generation of home-grown insurrectionists in Ireland, culminating in the 1798 Rebellion and then the 1803 United Irishmen Rebellion led by Robert Emmet. British success in suppressing these revolutions caused some politicians to believe that uprisings could even be beneficial, if they took place in a limited fashion, as rebels would come to the fore and could be dealt with more easily. In 1813, for example, Charles Whitworth, Lord Lieutenant of Ireland, wrote to Peel arguing that 'another revolution would be beneficial to the country ... it would lead to an unfortunate loss of life, but the results would be favourable to the tranquillity of the country'.[8] Nevertheless, the fear of similar uprisings prompted the British government to embark on an extensive programme of building military barracks throughout Ireland. In 1807 the Duke of Wellington, Sir Arthur Wellesley, remarked that the construction of garrisons 'afforded a prospect of security', despite the expenditure incurred by governments and landlords.[9] Aside from the fear of further revolution, England was at war with France and invasion by Napoleon's army was a real possibility, given that French naval ships had landed soldiers at Bantry Bay in 1786 and Killala Bay in 1798.[10] To guard against invasion, over forty Martello towers were constructed around the coast, and between 1789 and 1814 the number of military garrisons in Ireland increased from 40,000 to 225,000.[11] The army intensely disliked performing policing duties. Major-General G. C. Mundy of the 43rd Regiment of Foot wrote, when garrisoned in Cork during 1834, that he had 'no patience with playing police in this unsociable country'.[12] To reduce the burden on the army during the turbulent years of the late eighteenth and early nineteenth centuries, organisations of voluntary, non-professional soldiers were formed with the creation of a militia in 1793 and a yeomanry in 1796. Both organisations carried out quasi-policing functions, but proved to be frequently partisan in nature and less than efficient.[13]

In 1785 the London and Westminster Police Bill came before Parliament in an effort to address the escalating problem of crime in the city. The bill was defeated, however, having met opposition from influential members of society, who were wary of the increased powers it would give to the government and the significant costs associated with the establishment and maintenance of a police force. The following year, a similar measure for the city of Dublin was passed by the Irish parliament, which established the Dublin Metropolitan Police (DMP) and the term 'police' was enshrined in legislation for the first time in the United Kingdom.[14] The Dublin Police Act defined the boundaries of the city as the area within the Circular Road and Phoenix Park, and legislated for an unarmed police force within the capital.[15] While this model of urban policing had been innovative when first introduced, by the early part of the nineteenth century it was in need of reform. One magistrate once refused to parade the force in daylight, believing that 'they would excite so much ridicule of the people that there is a risk of their very appearance causing a disturbance'.[16] The DMP remained unarmed throughout its existence, and was subsumed into Garda Síochána na hÉireann under the Police Forces Amalgamation Act of 1925.

Outside of the city of Dublin, the Peace Preservation Act of 1814 introduced the Peace Preservation Force (PPF), a mounted quasi-military constabulary. Prior to this initiative, a rudimentary system of rural policing had existed in Ireland for centuries. Baronial constables, night watchmen and primarily the military, including the yeomanry and the militia, had been responsible for the preservation of law and order. The PPF was a nascent version of the constabulary that was to follow. The force was deployed to counties categorised as 'disturbed' when local magistrates requested that the Lord Lieutenant proclaim the area to be in a state of disorder. The costs of deploying the PPF were defrayed locally by landowners. In command of the new force was a full-time stipendiary magistrate, appointed by and answerable to the government. To fill the rank and file of the PPF, Peel stated his preference that they should be 'disbanded sergeants and veteran soldiers who were Roman Catholics'.[17]

On the first deployment of the force, to the Barony of Middlethird in County Tipperary on 6 September 1814, twenty-one heavily armed former cavalry sergeants arrived in the town of Cashel on horseback. As a former Member of Parliament for the area, Peel was aware that Tipperary had a long tradition of rebellion and lawlessness, which he remarked on when writing to the Lord Lieutenant in 1813:

> You can have no idea of the moral depravation of the lower orders in that county ... in fidelity towards each other they are unexampled, as they are in their sanguinary disposition and fearlessness of the consequences.[18]

Peel realised, however, that using the army in a policing role was problematical and in 1814 he informed Parliament that 'the frequent use of soldiers in that manner made the people look upon them as their adversaries rather than as their protectors'.[19] Shortly after the establishment of the PPF, agrarian-related fighting between secret societies in Tipperary such as the Shanavests and the Caravats was suppressed by the force under the command of Major Richard Willcocks, based in Cashel.[20] In 1822 the PPF was again deployed to deal with another outbreak of agrarian violence in Tipperary. The success of the force in 'patrolling, detection and gathering evidence' in the county caused the Lord Lieutenant, the Marquis of Wellesley, to write to Peel commending the actions of the police led by Major Willcocks.[21]

The PPF served a useful purpose by introducing the concept of a professional, disciplined police force to rural Ireland, and while consideration was given to extending the force to other counties in Ireland, Peel instead brought a bill to Parliament on 5 August 1822 that established the County Constabulary. This act formed four provincial police forces in Ireland, with an authorised strength of over 5,000 men. The introduction of organised policing to rural Ireland confirmed the determination of the British government to bring law and order to the countryside in the period following the Act of Union.[22] Policing and the police became integral to the social and political history of this turbulent era, thus laying the foundations for intergenerational violence.[23] The revolutionary credentials of Tipperary in 1919 were firmly rooted in the tradition of agrarian violence and secret societies in previous generations, and the 'disposition of the Irish peasant class towards organised crime and disturbance'.[24]

The County Constabulary was reformed under the Constabulary (Ireland) Act of 1836, which amalgamated the four provincial police forces into one national structure under the command of an inspector general based in Dublin Castle. The castle would remain as the headquarters of the Irish Constabulary until 1922, and was a powerful physical symbol of government, described by the liberal politician and historian John Morley as 'the best machine that has ever been invented for governing a country against its will'.[25] The French author Louis Paul-Dubois prosaically defined the castle as 'a world in itself, a city within a city. It is at once the palace of the viceroy, a military barrack, the seat of administration, and the office of the secret police ... omnipotent and omniscient'.[26]

The Irish Constabulary initially adopted a military bearing, being equipped with carbines and bayonets, and wore a dark green uniform, similar to that of the Rifle Brigade Regiment of the British Army. In a letter to the Chief Secretary, Viscount Edward Cardwell, in 1860, Under-Secretary Thomas Larcom warned of the danger in allowing the police to be too militaristic in nature, arguing that it was very difficult to keep a force of that nature 'in the right middle way in a country whose social condition has changed and is changing year by year ... it demands increasing watchfulness'.[27] Policemen were required to live in barracks and actively discouraged from marrying. Discipline was rigidly enforced and regulations prohibited men from serving in their native county or in any county where they had relatives.

The constabulary gradually became the 'public face of government in Ireland ... responsible for everything from the muzzling of a dog to the suppression of a rebellion'.[28] This integration, which has been categorised by some historians as the 'domestication' of the RIC, took place primarily after 1860 when the force became more representative of the society that it policed.[29] The RIC manual of regulations made it clear that it was the constable's job to acquire a thorough knowledge of his district and 'good relations with the locals made this easier'.[30] The magazine of the force, the *Constabulary Gazette*, frequently highlighted the importance of acquiring local knowledge, and offered the opinion that, on the appearance of any suspicious stranger in any sub-district, the constabulary should 'not rest till they have discovered who or what he is'.[31] County inspectors were instructed not to recommend for promotion any man who was wanting in civility and helpfulness to people making inquiries or in difficulty.[32]

In 1864 Inspector General Shaw Kennedy brought substantial changes to the force by introducing a new rank system and a comprehensive written disciplinary code. The mandatory transfer of policemen to counties where they had no prior connection became a key feature of service in the RIC. Shaw Kennedy stated that 'men had to be removed from their local connections ... amongst whom no policeman can in this country, for any length of time, impartially discharge his duty'.[33] The stringent disciplinary regulations within the force subsequently softened under the tenure of Sir Andrew Reed, a key figure in the history of Irish policing who served as inspector general from 1885 to 1900. By 1919, therefore, the force contained a substantial body of experienced, reliable policemen with families to support who had served for lengthy periods in their districts. The steady process of domestication and integration ensured that, despite the perception of the RIC as a paramilitary police force, when confronted with a volunteer army of young and dedicated guerrilla fighters in 1919, it was unable to cope.

In 1848 the devastation brought by the ongoing Famine, combined with the traditions of agrarian violence and allegiance to secret societies, led to the abortive Young Ireland Rebellion of 1848, which had its epicentre at Ballingarry in south Tipperary. The Young Irelanders were a nationalist group of middle-class university graduates led by William Smith O'Brien, Member of Parliament for County Limerick. Other key members included Thomas Davis, Charles Gavan

Duffy and John Blake Dillon. The Young Ireland movement had its own newspaper, *The Nation,* which was founded in 1842 to promote the idea of nationalism and campaign for the repeal of the Act of Union.[34] Inspired by rebellions that were taking place throughout Europe, including the declaration of a republic in France, the Young Irelanders denounced the government for not doing enough to end the misery of the Famine, and made plans for a similar uprising in Ireland.

In July 1848 the government imprisoned Young Irelanders without trial, forcing the hand of the movement's leaders. From 23–29 July of that year, Smith O'Brien, Dillon and Thomas Francis Meagher travelled through counties Wexford, Kilkenny and Tipperary hoping to inspire tenant farmers and tradesmen to revolt. When they reached the village of Ballingarry in south Tipperary, a confrontation took place between the Young Irelanders and forty-six members of the constabulary who had come to arrest them under the command of Sub-Inspector Thomas Trant. When the police realised that they were outnumbered, they barricaded themselves in a large two-storey farmhouse owned by a local widow, Mrs Margaret McCormack. A tense stand-off ensued between the rebels and the police. Shots were fired by the constabulary and returned by the rebels, inflicting casualties on both sides. A local Roman Catholic priest, Father Fitzgerald, tried to mediate between the parties, but police reinforcements arrived, forcing the rebels to flee the area, thus effectively ending the Young Ireland movement. Smith O'Brien, Meagher, Terence Bellew MacManus and Patrick O'Donohue were captured and tried for high treason, for which they were found guilty. The jury recommended clemency, and while they were initially sentenced to death, this was later commuted by Act of Parliament to penal imprisonment for life in Van Diemen's Land (modern-day Tasmania), Australia. There, they were joined by other Young Irelanders including John Martin, Kevin Izod O'Doherty and John Mitchell. Twenty-one local men from Ballingarry and surrounding parishes in south Tipperary were also arrested and imprisoned in Ireland. The so-called 1848 Rising was an abject failure in military terms and, as stated by Robert Kee, it was not 'in any practical sense a rising at all, nor until the very last minute was it ever intended to be one'.[35] It was a significant event nonetheless for later generations of Tipperary nationalists. Many militants were inspired by the events in Ballingarry and subsequent failed uprisings, not only in Tipperary but elsewhere in Ireland.

Following on from this tradition of secret societies and agrarian conflict, Tipperary became a fertile area for recruitment to the new IRB/Fenian movement established in 1858.[36] It grew steadily and, despite internal divisions, the leadership set a date of 5 March 1867 for an armed rebellion in Ireland. The military inadequacy of the Fenians, combined with bad weather, intelligence received from the American government and the overwhelming strength of the military and constabulary response, ensured that the rising was over almost as soon as it had begun. Tipperary did see upheaval, however – particularly in the countryside between Clonmel and Tipperary town. A railway line was damaged and houses were raided for arms by the police. RIC barracks in Emly and Gortavoher were attacked, but the police were able to repel the Fenians. Responding to reports that 'the Galtee Mountains were swarming with insurgents', large parties of military and police carried out extensive searches throughout the Tipperary countryside. Of the 1,086 Fenians arrested in Ireland in 1867, the majority came from County Tipperary, with Clonmel described as a 'hotbed of Fenianism' by the local police inspector.[37] Following the 1867 Rebellion many of its leaders were captured, tried and initially sentenced to death, but this was usually commuted to deportation to a penal colony.

The uprising was a military failure, but the Fenian movement gave nationalists a new sense of purpose and ensured that future generations would continue to aspire to separation from Britain. The influence of the Fenians continued to be felt over the next half century, culminating with the 1916 Easter Rising, which kept alive the tradition of armed revolt.[38] The 1867 Rebellion was also a significant event in the history of the Irish Constabulary. For its role in suppressing the Fenians, Queen Victoria issued instructions that the force would henceforth be known as the Royal Irish Constabulary, and thus entitled to have the harp and crown as the badge of the force. Several policemen, including Constable Patrick Derwan from Emly and Constable Martin Scurry from Gortavoher, both in south Tipperary, were awarded the constabulary medal for bravery.[39] By 1871, Tipperary had become heavily policed due to its radical nationalist composition. It had the highest policeman-to-population ratio of the seventy county forces throughout Ireland and England, with a ratio of 1:194 based on a population of 216,210. The county with the lowest police-to-population ratio was Shropshire, with a ratio of 1:1,752. There were 1,600 police barracks throughout Ireland, ranging from a low of sixteen in County Londonderry to a high of 153 in Tipperary.[40]

During the period of the Land War and the consequent resurgence in agrarian-related conflict in the late nineteenth century, the RIC was heavily involved in policing Land League meetings and evictions. During a speech made in Ennis, County Clare, on 19 September 1880, Charles Stewart Parnell, leader of the Land League and Member of Parliament for Meath, expressed his views on how a boycott against the police should be implemented. He exhorted people to put policemen into a 'moral Coventry, by isolating him from the rest of his kind as if he was a leper of old ... you must show him your detestation of the crime he has committed'.[41] Intimidation and boycotting of policemen and their families thus became effective strategies during this period.[42] The socio-economic background of the average constable was modest. Most were the sons of small farmers, shopkeepers, tradesmen or artisans. Members of the RIC used the stability of their employment to pay the rent on their parents' farms, thus protecting them from the threat of eviction. For the remainder of its existence, however, the force would be stigmatised by its association with agrarian-related policing duties, which placed onerous demands on the police. Even the usually pro-nationalist, anti-government *The Freeman's Journal* described the position of the RIC in 1882 as 'intolerable'.[43] The strain of performing such duties for lengthy periods eventually led to an unprecedented situation, in which several hundred policemen from a body renowned for rigid discipline and dedicated service briefly engaged in a public protest in 1882 for improved pay and conditions.[44] The tactical use of intimidation and boycotting by Land War leaders, particularly Parnell, fulfilled the dual purpose of appeasing both the advocates of physical-force republicanism and those who preferred more passive resistance.[45] It was a strategy that would be repeated to significant effect when hostilities erupted in 1919, with deadly consequences for hundreds of members of the RIC.

By the turn of the twentieth century the RIC was divided by class, religion and social status, reflective of the society that it policed. Junior officers joined the force as cadets and graduated as third-class district inspectors, the lowest officer rank. Cadets were almost exclusively Protestant, and expected to be 'officers and gentlemen' in a similar fashion to military officers. They could also use the title 'Esquire' after their names in all official correspondence. The religious composition of the force also mirrored that of Irish society and, consistently, more than 70 per cent of the force was Roman Catholic.[46] Promotion to the officer corps, however, which included any rank above that of head constable, was almost impossible for any Roman Catholic to achieve until well into the twentieth century.

In the course of the 1916 Rising, fourteen RIC members were killed and a further twenty-three injured. Eight policemen were killed in a single ambush at Kilmoon, near Ashbourne in County Meath. In Tipperary, Sergeant Thomas O'Rourke and Constable John Hurley were shot dead by Volunteer Michael O'Callaghan when they tried to arrest him at Lisvernane in the Glen of Aherlow. O'Callaghan subsequently escaped to America, only returning in 1922 after the cessation of hostilities.[47] Despite these significant events, as an organisation the force was unprepared for the escalation of militant nationalism and the associated growth in intimidation and violence that followed thereafter.[48]

When conflict broke out in 1919 the structure of the RIC in County Tipperary owed much to the policing necessities and agrarian violence of previous generations. The number of RIC barracks in Ireland had steadily decreased from 1,600 in 1871 to 1,397 in 1913, with the most heavily policed areas being the south and the west of the country. The number of barracks in Tipperary declined from 153 in 1871 to 79 by 1913, and the county had a policeman-to-population ratio of 1:330, as compared to a ratio of 1:732 for County Down (see appendices 1 and 2 for a list of RIC barracks).[49] As secessionists reorganised and prepared to intensify the conflict, the RIC had a total of 12,900 policemen located throughout the thirty-two counties of Ireland, a strength that was largely unchanged from the 1852 figure of 11,286.[50] By contrast, the strength of the Irish Volunteers was estimated by the RIC to be 112,000 just before the outbreak of conflict in 1919.[51]

Nationalist historiography frequently depicts the RIC as a paramilitary police force that ruthlessly suppressed the people of Ireland on behalf of a colonial oppressor. Writing about the force in 1937, fifteen years after it had been disbanded, the nationalist historian Dorothy Macardle argued that the key role of its members was to investigate, suppress and report disaffection of every kind, rather than perform routine policing duties. She also contended that it was indicative of the 'extremities to which the Irish people had been reduced' that the government was able to constitute the force entirely of Irishmen.[52] In 1952 the historian, civil servant and separatist P. S. O'Hegarty wrote of the RIC that the loyalty of the force lay not with Ireland but with England, and by virtue of that loyalty, they 'bullied, terrorised and, when ordered, murdered their own people without compunction for nearly a hundred years'.[53] To members of the militant separatist movement, the RIC represented the physical and symbolic embodiment of British rule in Ireland. For some periods of its existence, the constabulary did function as an armed quasi-military force due to the political circumstances that prevailed at those particular times. By the first decade of the twentieth century, however, the RIC was an indigenous civil police force, which habitually policed without arms and carried out routine policing functions.

Many nationalists based their loathing of the RIC on their perception of the involvement of the police in dealing with the agrarian violence of the previous century, or their presence at the scene of evictions during the Land War in the late nineteenth century. Eamon O'Duibhir, a Tipperary member of the IRB and IRA, spoke of his anger towards policemen 'protecting the evictors throwing the poor people of their own race out of their homes'.[54] Even hardline separatists such as O'Duibhir, however, acknowledged that by 1919, the RIC as an organisation contained disparate types within its ranks. He categorised four distinct groupings of policemen, as he saw them. Firstly, there were 'decent Irishmen' who provided information to the IRA. Then, a percentage that feared poverty too much to leave the constabulary, but avoided conflict. He characterised a third group of 'decent men loyal to Britain' and finally a 'percentage of hellishly anti-Irish ruffians who were the guides and masked killers of the British murder gangs'.[55] O'Duibhir does not refer to the religion or class of policemen, but his recollections make it clear that at local level, personal animosity and past relationships between individual policemen and Volunteers were commonplace. Aspirant revolutionaries such as Dan Breen and Seán Treacy in Tipperary and Tom Barry in Cork believed that the constabulary was the 'real power behind the British grip on Ireland', and had been responsible for the collapse of the 1916 Rising outside of Dublin. Breen saw the RIC as 'a pack of deserters, spies and hirelings ... the eyes and ears of British intelligence, and as natives of the country, they had an intimate knowledge of the people and ferreted out vital information for the army of occupation'.[56]

Historians such as Brewer, Lowe and Malcolm disagree with Breen and suggest that it is not unusual in post-colonial societies for scholars to look closely and perhaps somewhat more sympathetically at those citizens who served the British Empire or other 'occupying power', such as civil servants, magistrates and soldiers.[57] Given the passage of time and the transition of the RIC from living memory into history, it is opportune to give a more balanced view of events of the period and the role of the RIC in those events. The military historian M. L. R. Smith suggests that the notion of colonial subjugation is the strongest theme in Irish nationalism, and that it forms the 'central hypothesis of republican political analysis'.[58] Stephen Ellis argues that the perception of the British-Irish relationship as a colonial one is merely a matter of opinion, as colonialism as a concept was 'developed by its modern opponents and constitutes a value judgement which cannot be challenged on its own grounds'.[59] The characterisation of the RIC as a colonial police force can therefore be pejorative. It is clear from the analysis of historians such as Brewer, Lowe and Malcolm that while it suited the purposes of militant nationalists to portray policemen as mercenaries, the rationale behind joining the RIC was usually quite unsophisticated. It lay in the acquisition of a secure job with prospects and a pension at the end of service. In the heat of conflict, however, and following the introduction of the Black and Tans and Auxiliary Division, bitterness, enmity and revenge became key factors for men on both sides.

In contrast to the body of literature that exists on the IRA and the period between 1913 and 1923, there is a dearth of material about the RIC. As key protagonists, the question arises as to why the experiences of RIC members have thus far been largely omitted from the historiography of the period. Policing during the revolution is a contentious subject, which requires ongoing research and debate. A complete history of the force is yet to be written; the sole official volume, *A History of the Royal Irish Constabulary* by District Inspector Robert Curtis, was published in 1871. This work concludes with the 1867 Phoenix Park ceremony that saw the Constabulary of Ireland being renamed as the Royal Irish Constabulary. It is far from a complete history of the force. Nonetheless, it gives some interesting insights into the foundation and earliest deployments of the constabulary.

The autobiographies and memoirs of RIC officers provide useful insight into the inner workings of the constabulary. The memoir of John M. Regan, a Catholic officer in the RIC, covers some key events such as the 1916 Rising and Listowel police mutiny.[60] However, he is circumspect about some of the actions carried out by men under his command. Following the disbandment of the RIC in 1922, Regan went on to serve in the Royal Ulster Constabulary (RUC), and retired in 1948 as its highest ranking Catholic officer, after a forty-year career.

Thomas Fennell joined the RIC in 1875 aged eighteen, and by 1897 had reached the rank of head constable, the highest non-commissioned rank in the force.[61] Fennell had already spent many years in retirement by the time the conflict began in 1919. His autobiography displays his pride in having served in the RIC and also his inherent nationalist sympathies, which he states were shared by most members of the force with whom he served. A well read, articulate and ambitious man, Fennell worked his way steadily upwards in the force, and passed the written examinations for promotion to the rank of district inspector. When he reached the age of forty-eight, however, he was no longer eligible for promotion, as this was the upper age limit for advancement, a regulation that was deeply unpopular among the Roman Catholic majority of the force. His memoir notes his experiences as a Roman Catholic vying for promotion. It provides a valuable first-hand perspective of service in the RIC, but is hindered by a lack of contemporary references, and much of the content predates the revolutionary period.

With over forty years of service in the constabulary, Samuel Waters served in all four provinces. He was involved in the policing of key events such as the Fenian uprising of 1867, the Land War and the 1916 Rising. He followed his father and grandfather into the constabulary and achieved the rank of assistant inspector general. In his autobiography, Waters offers an interesting perspective on relationships with the community and the social and sporting benefits of being an RIC officer. While his reminiscences do not deal with the 1919–21 period, they nonetheless provide a unique insight due to the high rank that he held, and help to contextualise the role of the RIC in contemporary Irish society.[62]

The autobiography of Douglas V. Duff, who joined the Black and Tans in 1920 after serving in the Royal Navy, offers an alternative view to that of the regular RIC member. Arriving in Ireland, where he had spent much of his youth, Duff was posted to Mayo and Galway, where he was involved in numerous engagements with the IRA. Duff's credibility is hindered by his status as a prolific author of fiction; he wrote over one hundred books during his lifetime, many under pseudonyms, and perhaps brought some artistic licence to his memoirs. Nonetheless, he was well schooled in Irish affairs and believed the conflict to be a 'fratricidal civil war, the worst of all wars' rather than a war of rebellion against British rule in Ireland.[63]

A groundbreaking work on the RIC during the period of 1919 to 1922 is *The Royal Irish Constabulary: An Oral History* by John D. Brewer,[64] which is an important social history of the force. In 1990, Brewer conducted interviews with fifteen remaining survivors of the force, including two former Black and Tans, all of whom have since died. Brewer sheds new light on issues including the reasons why young men joined the RIC, station life, routine police work, policing in violent counties, serving alongside the Black and Tans, and the consequences of the force's disbandment. Oral history serves a useful function in allowing individuals' stories to be heard, but caution must be exercised as such recollections can be partisan in nature, and the passage of time can distort events. Brewer states that the oral testimony should stand by itself. Nonetheless, he offers the valid conclusion that the standards of entry to the force were greatly relaxed after 1919 and the membership of the RIC was largely depoliticised. He also shows that most policemen were unprepared and unfit for the role that the conflict thrust upon them. Routine policing functions and crime investigation carried on between 1919 and 1922, even in violent counties such as Tipperary. Brewer concludes that the RIC was forced to operate as a heavily armed entity in the latter years of its existence and while this model of policing was dictated by the prevailing circumstances, it was not one that the majority of the membership endorsed.

The 2006 work of Elizabeth Malcolm, *The Irish Policeman, 1822–1922*, draws on a wide range of sources, including correspondence between the author and over 200 descendants of policemen, along with unpublished memoirs and personal papers.[65] It offers valuable insight into how policemen lived and worked in Irish society. Malcolm concludes that service in the constabulary was an alternative to emigration for most members, and that policing was viewed as a job rather than a vocation.[66] *Police Casualties in Ireland 1919–22* by Richard Abbott lists all known RIC fatalities from the outbreak of conflict in 1919 until the disbandment of the force in 1922, giving a short biography of each policeman killed and the reported circumstances in which he died.[67] It is an incomplete record, however, as the full list of RIC fatalities may never be known. For example, Abbott lists eighteen policemen who disappeared between 1919 and 1922 who may have been abducted and killed by the IRA, but whose deaths were never claimed by that organisation or otherwise explained. He does, however, provide a clear insight into the reality of the conflict, chronologically identifying the humanity behind the statistics.

Voices and the Sound of Drums is the autobiography of Patrick Shea, the son of an RIC sergeant serving in Tipperary in 1920.[68] Shea's narrative focuses on the effect of the IRA campaign of boycotting and intimidation on policemen's families, and how they gradually became unsuspecting participants in the conflict. Given his family's experience, Shea admits that his judgement of the RIC is subjective, but concludes that his father stayed in the force during the conflict not because of allegiance to the King or the government, but because of a sense of loyalty to and comradeship with his fellow members of the force. Shea's autobiography is slightly dramatised, but much less so than the anonymously authored

Tales of the RIC, first published in 1921. This sensationalised narrative of incidents such as ambushes and barrack attacks is believed to have been written by a serving member of the force. As such, it provides a contemporary viewpoint of the conflict, but should be considered a work of fiction.[69]

The memoirs of high-ranking members of the force are another useful source of information. The 1924 two-volume memoir of General Sir Nevil Macready, Commander-in-Chief of British forces in Ireland from 1918 to 1920, provides military, policing and political insights into the War of Independence.[70] A career solider and former commissioner of the London Metropolitan Police, Macready was involved in the Truce negotiations and supervised the orderly withdrawal of British troops from Ireland in 1922. A similar memoir is that of Brigadier General Frank Crozier, who arrived in Ireland during July 1920 to take command of the Auxiliary Division. A former member of the Ulster Volunteer Force (UVF), he commanded the 36th Ulster Division during the Battle of the Somme in 1916. Following the robbery of a creamery in Kells and the looting of a grocery shop in Robinstown, both in County Meath, Crozier had five temporary cadets arrested, and a further twenty-one dismissed, believing that members of the Auxiliary Division were responsible for both crimes. Critical of the lack of military discipline among members of the Auxiliaries, when these men were reinstated by his superiors, Crozier resigned as commander of the division in February 1921, and was replaced by Brigadier General E. A. Wood. Written in 1932, Crozier's memoirs give an understanding of division's activities and the government-sanctioned policy of official reprisals in response to IRA violence.[71] By that time, however, Crozier had become a noted pacifist and a critic of the establishment, which should be borne in mind when analysing his retrospective view of the events of 1920 and 1921.

David Leeson deals at length with the circumstances of Crozier's resignation in *The Black and Tans: British Police and Auxiliaries in the Irish War of Independence*.[72] Leeson also contextualises the British government's responsibility for reprisals in Ireland, and justifiably argues that it was inappropriate for the British government to deploy police in an insurgency situation. He accurately counters the stereotypical view that members of the Black and Tans and Auxiliary Division were criminals released from English jails, and concludes that the British government and IRA had one thing in common from 1919 to 1921: neither objected in principle to reprisals. Leeson's analysis augments and supersedes the 1959 work of Richard Bennett, *The Black and Tans,* which is hampered by a misleading title as it is not specifically about the Black and Tans, but is instead a more general history of the 1919–22 period, and suffers from inadequate references and the lack of a detailed bibliography.[73]

In February 1920, RIC Constable Jeremiah Mee acted as a representative for discontented policemen during an incident that subsequently became known as 'the Listowel police mutiny'. His experiences are recounted in *The Memoirs of Constable Jeremiah Mee RIC* by J. A. Gaughan.[74] During the mutiny, the British Army was refused access to the RIC barracks and several policemen resigned in protest, following a speech given by the divisional police commissioner for Munster, Colonel Gerald Bryce Ferguson Smyth. While visiting the station, Smyth stated that the martial law then in force in Munster could be used to allow the RIC and military to engage in a ruthless campaign against the IRA and even if innocent people were killed as a result, no policeman would be held accountable. Mee protested and called Smyth 'a murderer', following which Smyth ordered Mee's arrest, but no other RIC members present were willing to obey his order. Following an impasse, Mee and several other constables left the barracks and resigned from the force. Following his resignation, Mee made contact with IRA members and was summoned to Dublin where he briefed senior Sinn Féin figures, including Michael Collins and Countess Markievicz, on the circumstances of the Listowel mutiny. Mee was subsequently employed in the Department of Labour of the first Dáil, and formed an association to encourage RIC members to resign. Bryce Ferguson Smyth was shot dead by the IRA in Cork city on 17 July 1920.

David Neligan joined the Dublin Metropolitan Police in 1917, becoming a member of its political section, G Division, in 1919.[75] However, he resigned from the force in 1920 at the behest of his brother Maurice, an IRA member. Michael Collins, a friend of Maurice Neligan, persuaded David to re-join the DMP and provide intelligence to the IRA, which he did until the Truce. Neligan went on to serve as director of intelligence for the Free State army and also as a chief superintendent of the Garda Síochána. While Neligan's memoir, *The Spy in the Castle,* does not refer to the conflict in Tipperary, he does acknowledge that many policemen serving in the RIC and DMP helped the IRA in a variety of ways, which is indicative of the divided loyalties of many Irish policemen. Neligan knew that information he provided to the IRA would result in the deaths of his colleagues from G Division, but he stated in later life that he acted as a double agent because of his nationalist beliefs and his admiration for Michael Collins.

Dan Breen is a notable character in the narrative of the revolution in Tipperary. Born in 1894 at Donohill in south Tipperary, Breen grew up steeped in the nationalist folklore of previous generations, which centred on the Famine and the Land War. A volatile character, Breen became immersed in the Volunteer movement and was heavily influenced by his friendship with Seán Treacy. Both were angered that their planned involvement in the 1916 Rising had been cancelled when Tipperary Volunteers were stood down by Volunteer leader Eoin MacNeill, and their determination to redress this led to the planning and execution of the Soloheadbeg ambush of 21 January 1919. In his autobiography, which was first published in 1924, Breen narrates many of the incidents and ambushes in which he was involved as a member of the Third Brigade of the Tipperary IRA.[76] While this memoir is regarded as a classic, it differs substantially from the comprehensive statements made in later life by Breen to the Bureau of Military History. Such discrepancies illustrate the caution that must be exercised when reading memoirs and witness statements. The 1945 biography of Seán Treacy, a close associate of Breen and another key figure in the Third Brigade of the Tipperary IRA, provides useful information about the rationale and execution of the Soloheadbeg ambush, which is considered by many historians to be a pivotal event in Irish history.[77]

The primary sources for this book are the RIC records of the United Kingdom National Archives at Kew in London.[78] These registers contain the service records of policemen between 1816 and 1922 and are searchable by the individual service numbers allocated to RIC recruits upon enlistment.[79] They also contain personal information including age, height, religion, native county, previous trade, etc. As these records were maintained throughout the careers of RIC members, they also contain details of transfers, promotions, marriages, lengths of service, retirements and deaths. The archive provides an invaluable social history of the RIC from foundation to disbandment. The Paymaster General Series 48 series is especially relevant to the disbandment of the RIC, as it contains pension or disbandment details for men who served in the force between 1873 and 1922. Each policeman was required to complete a 'form of option' when the RIC was disbanded, giving their intended future address.[80] The disbandment of the RIC came at a huge financial cost to the British Exchequer, which became liable for pensions, commutations and other expenses connected with the disbandment of the force.[81]

Of particular relevance to this book are the Dublin Castle records.[82] These are the annals of the British administration in Ireland prior to 1922. Most of this material relates directly or indirectly to the methods adopted by the authorities, using civil and military forces, to combat the efforts of nationalist organisations to secure Irish independence. Commencing in 1795, the archive includes material on various nationalist movements, including Ribbonism, the United Irish League and Sinn Féin, as well as the monthly reports of district and county inspectors of the RIC from 1919 to 1922. These reports categorised crimes as either 'crime ordinary' or 'crime special', the latter meaning that they were believed to be politically motivated. By 1919 the Special Branch of the RIC had become outmoded and ineffectual, primarily acting as a repository for information submitted by uniformed members throughout Ireland. Attacks on policemen were regarded as 'ordinary' crimes and categorised accordingly, and militant nationalists were regarded as criminals rather than revolutionaries.

As reports were submitted on a county by county basis, incidents that took place in Tipperary, such as ambushes and barrack attacks, are covered in detail. The 'weekly outrage reports', first introduced in 1920, list incidents where policemen were killed or injured and police pensioners or RIC candidates were threatened or intimidated.[83] These records provide a valuable chronological and contemporary outline of individual incidents by county. Due caution must be exercised when referring to this material, however, as the collection contains propaganda reports, and the exact circumstances of some individual incidents were misreported for a variety of reasons. For this book, source material has been cross-referenced with contemporary newspaper reports, IRA veteran statements and other material to ensure the accuracy of information when referring to the specifics of ambushes and the circumstances surrounding the deaths of policemen in Tipperary. Other records in the RIC collection include correspondence with the Treasury, intelligence notes, and papers relating to RIC involvement in combating disturbances throughout Ireland between 1916 and 1922.[84]

Another significant source of information is the archive of witness statements of IRA Volunteers from the three Tipperary brigades, located at the Military Archives in Cathal Brugha Barracks, Dublin. These statements were made during the 1950s to officers of the Irish Defence Forces representing the Bureau of Military History. The bureau was established in January 1947 by Oscar Traynor TD, then Minister for Defence and a former captain in the Irish Volunteers. The creation of the bureau gave individuals involved in key events from 1913 to 1923 a chance to narrate their own detailed personal accounts of the conflict. Statements were not released to academics, researchers or the wider population until the last surviving person who had made a statement had died. The collection contains 1,773 witness statements, including some made by RIC members who had worked as double agents for the IRA during the conflict. Also included in the bureau collection are 334 sets of contemporary documents, such as diaries, pamphlets, photographs, letters, dispatches, drawings and sketches, posters, legal documents and newspaper clippings. The release of this material, while resulting in a substantial increase in the amount of literature relating to republicanism and the IRA in particular, has not been without controversy. Some files, for example, contain blank sections where statements were redacted under the provision of the National Archives Act of 1986 on the basis that their release 'might cause distress or danger to living persons on the grounds that they contain information about individuals ... or might lead to action for damages or defamation'.[85] IRA witness statements provide excellent primary source material, albeit with the caveat that some can be self-serving. The statements were made over thirty years after the events had taken place, meaning that caution should be exercised regarding the accuracy of such recollections. Notwithstanding these reservations, the statements provide valuable first-hand perspectives from people who took an active part in the conflict.

This volume begins by dealing with the period from December 1918 to March 1920. Tensions between the RIC and the Irish Volunteers escalated following the 1916 Rising, and on 21 January 1919 an ambush took place near Soloheadbeg quarry in south Tipperary. Two RIC constables escorting a shipment of explosives, James McDonnell and Patrick O'Connell, were shot dead by members of the Third

Brigade of the Tipperary IRA. While some RIC members had been killed since 1916, there is consensus among many historians and academics that the Soloheadbeg event largely prompted the 1919–21 conflict, and is therefore worthy of the detailed study it is afforded in these pages. The first chapter ends with the arrival of police reinforcements to Ireland in the form of the Black and Tans and Auxiliary Division, a development that was to have profound and lasting consequences, both for the civilian population and for the RIC.

The second chapter examines the most violent period of the conflict in County Tipperary, March to December 1920. As fighting intensified, a parallel campaign of intimidation and boycotting of RIC members and their families took place. Both sides engaged in reprisals and counter-reprisals, and neither had a monopoly on atrocities. The third chapter analyses the period from January to July 1921 when, after lengthy and secretive negotiations involving intermediaries, a truce was agreed between the British government and the IRA. Fourteen policemen had been killed in Tipperary since the start of 1921, but for members of the RIC in the county, relief at the cessation of hostilities was soon replaced with apprehension as to what the future might bring.

The post-Truce period from July 1921 to August 1922, which saw the signing of the Anglo-Irish Treaty and the disbandment of the RIC, is the subject of the fourth chapter. In the aftermath of the Truce, an uneasy peace prevailed, and in Tipperary, as in other counties, the RIC was confined to its barracks, with Truce liaison officers appointed by both sides to monitor proceedings and report on any apparent breaches. To the frustration of RIC members, the IRA was formally acknowledged, giving the militant movement the status it sought, and its members appeared openly wearing military uniform in public. The implications of the Anglo-Irish Treaty for the RIC, and how the disbandment of the force unfolded in Tipperary and other counties, are outlined in detail. To manage the significant logistical task of disbanding the RIC in its entirety, the British government established a resettlement branch to assist former policemen and their families to relocate elsewhere in the Empire. The cost of assisted passage to other countries, pensions and compensation placed a substantial burden on the British government, which retained the resettlement branch until 1928.[86] The conclusion contains statistical analyses of the level of violence in Tipperary in comparison to other counties in Munster, which was the most violent province in Ireland between 1919 and 1921. The conclusion covers the aftermath of disbandment and the establishment of a new police force to replace the RIC, An Garda Síochána. It will be argued that the military campaign waged by the IRA against the RIC, while termed an Anglo-Irish conflict, or War of Independence, was in fact more analogous to a civil war.[87]

An RIC constable at the RIC Depot, Phoenix Park, 1920, in 'walking out' dress, which includes swagger stick and gloves. *(Courtesy of the Garda Photographic Section).*

1

'Six Dead Policemen': The Soloheadbeg Ambush and its Consequences

'That the harp of green Erin may never be without a string while there is a gut in a peeler.'[1]

In the immediate aftermath of the 1916 Rising the war correspondent H. W. Nevinson shrewdly predicted that the decision to execute the key figures behind the Rising, including Patrick Pearse and James Connolly, would generate huge sympathy for their cause. Writing in *Atlantic* magazine, Nevinson said 'we execute a worthless rebel, and for Ireland a heroic saint emerges from the felon's grave'.[2] In Tipperary, there initially seemed to be little public support for the Rising, with the *Tipperary Star* describing it as 'inexplicable imbecility – how men could embark on such a desperate enterprise passes common-sense comprehension. It is the old story … everything lost, nothing gained.'[3] The execution of the leaders of the Rising radically changed public perception, however. Thurles Volunteer James Leahy later recalled that 'the men who had lost or risked their lives in the Rising were now being regarded as heroes'.[4]

While Tipperary Volunteers did not take part in the Rising itself, Sergeant Thomas Rourke and Constable John Hurley of the RIC were shot dead on 25 April 1916 while trying to arrest Volunteer Michael O'Callaghan for making a seditious speech near Tipperary town. O'Callaghan went on the run and fled to America. For militants, including Dan Breen and Seán Treacy, O'Callaghan gained iconic status and was regarded as 'having saved the name of Tipperary during Easter week' for his actions.[5] Radicals had come to the conclusion that their aims could only be achieved militarily.[6] Despite this, in the immediate aftermath of the Rising overt Volunteer activity diminished and almost 2,000 men were interned.[7]

The public empathy after the executions of the 1916 leaders was capitalised upon, however, and the Volunteers gradually reorganised, increasing in number and engaging in open acts of defiance. During late 1916 and early 1917 those arrested after the Rising were released and returned home to rapturous receptions from supporters in their home counties. In 1917 Sinn Féin clubs and new Irish Volunteer companies were formed in Tipperary, and membership and activity greatly increased.[8] In August 1917 Éamon de Valera visited Tipperary town following his victory in east Clare, where he had been elected as a Sinn Féin Member of Parliament. A large crowd of Volunteers assembled and, in defiance of an official proclamation, paraded wearing Volunteer uniforms and carrying hurleys in place of rifles. One Volunteer recalled that relatives of the soldiers who were fighting in Europe 'flung rotten eggs and various classes of filth' at them, and scuffles took place, but that the RIC, apparently considering discretion the better part of valour, made no attempt to interfere.[9] From that point forward parades in Tipperary were held openly and in defiance of RIC efforts to prevent them. In December 1917 a military intelligence officer described the growing and increasingly militant nationalist movement as 'peculiarly well disciplined, in comparison with similar political organisations in the past'. He went on to say that drunkenness was almost unknown among those implicated, and was apparently dealt with severely. He found this to be 'in sharp contrast to the usual state of things in similar movements'.[10]

Tipperary proved to be fertile ground for recruitment to the militant movement. During the conscription crisis of early 1918, parades and field exercises were frequently held and plans made for the acquirement of arms. In January 1918 IRA headquarters formed brigades to replace the previous inefficient command structure, whereby each company reported directly to IRA General Headquarters (GHQ) in Dublin. In Tipperary, three brigades were formed: the First Brigade (north Tipperary), Second Brigade (mid-Tipperary) and Third Brigade (south Tipperary). Brigade officers and staff were elected by the membership, and Volunteers such as Seán Gaynor from Tipperary believed that the organisation was gradually becoming an effective military force.[11] Despite the December 1918 electoral success of Sinn Féin, which saw it take 73 parliamentary seats out of a possible 105, many Volunteers had grown frustrated with politics and were anxious to continue the struggle for independence that had begun in 1916. In south Tipperary, Seán Treacy chose not to take command of the new brigade, despite his prominence and strong belief in physical-force nationalism. The role went instead to Séamus Robinson from Belfast, a Gaelic League and Volunteer activist. Robinson, Dan Breen, Seán Treacy and Seán Hogan became known to their comrades as 'the big four' of the Third Tipperary Brigade, and while Robinson was respected for having taken part in the 1916 Rising, he recalled experiencing problems with the other men, who all came from the 'close, clannish world of south Tipperary'.[12]

In later years, militant nationalists in Tipperary, including Breen and Treacy, claimed they had come to the conclusion that 'positive military action was necessary'. They believed that 1916 was similar to 1798, referring to the United Irishmen Rebellion, which was viewed by them as a heroic enterprise that had also ended in failure. Treacy was insistent that something could be done to redeem this perceived failure and that Tipperary should 'distinguish itself in the national cause'. Treacy later recalled telling the others 'we have had enough of being pushed around and our men being killed by the enemy forces, and it is time that we did a bit of pushing around and killing on the other side'. The militants were frustrated that the events of 1916 had not led to a full-scale rebellion, and at their own lack of involvement in the Rising.[13]

The end of the conscription crisis of early 1918, allied to Sinn Féin's electoral success, meant that less militant members began to dominate the movement. During one brigade meeting at the end of 1918, Treacy wrote of his frustration at the lack of enthusiasm displayed by some Volunteers for drill and parades, and stated 'if this is the state of affairs, we will have to kill somebody and make the bloody enemy organise us.'[14] Individual RIC members deemed to be a particular threat were singled out for assassination, including District Inspector William Wilson in Templemore. Wilson joined the force in 1882 as a constable and rose steadily through the ranks, becoming district inspector for Templemore in 1912. Having served in the office of the inspector general at

RIC headquarters in Dublin Castle, Wilson had a significant knowledge of the Volunteer movement nationally, and particularly in north Tipperary. His assassination became a priority for local commandant James Leahy, who described Wilson as being in the 'black books because of his ruthless conduct in the treatment of Republicans'.[15] On 11 November 1918, the first Armistice Day, Volunteer Edward McGrath was ordered to travel to Templemore and kill Wilson if the opportunity arose. After waiting for several hours, McGrath saw Wilson and followed him with the intention of shooting him. However, the town was full of drunken soldiers celebrating the cessation of hostilities in France, and McGrath abandoned his assassination attempt, reasoning that Templemore was 'no place for a lone armed IRA man' on that occasion.

Richmond Barracks in Templemore was also targeted and in December 1918, Volunteers devised a plan to raid it and seize the contents of the arsenal. Richmond was a formidable complex capable of accommodating 1,200 soldiers, but intelligence was received that on Sunday afternoons it was customary for officers from the barracks to dine at Hickey's Hotel in the town while a military band played outside, and enlisted men went for walks in the surrounding countryside. This left the barracks virtually undefended. Plans were made to cut railway tracks and telephone lines before raiding the barracks, but, to the irritation of local Volunteers, IRA headquarters refused to approve the operation.[16]

In another step towards overt militancy, in January 1919 the name Irish Republican Army (IRA) was formally adopted by the Irish Volunteers. In Tipperary, as in a number of other counties, militants moved inexorably towards conflict with the police and military. Hard-line attitudes were fostered by the official organ of the Irish Volunteers, *An t-Óglách*. In November 1918, it editorialised that any civilian or soldier who plotted against the movement merited no consideration and should be 'killed without mercy or hesitation as opportunity offers'.[17] The Unionist MP and Colonial Office Minister Walter Long had been perceptive when he commented in 1918 that it was going to be a fair and square fight between the British government and Sinn Féin as to who was going to govern the country.[18] In January 1919 the RIC inspector general introduced a policy of compulsory retirement to rid the force of men who, for one reason or another, were no longer up to the required standard.[19] One former constable who was forced to retire under this provision later wrote that it had the effect of removing 'loyal, seasoned men and injuring morale'.[20]

The formation of an aspirational state commenced with the inaugural public meeting of Dáil Éireann in Dublin on 21 January 1919 at 3:30 p.m. This would prove to be a historic event, but just 100 miles to the south, at Soloheadbeg in south Tipperary, an IRA ambush took place that overshadowed those proceedings. Just before Christmas 1918 Breen, Treacy, Robinson and Hogan received information via an intercepted military communication that a shipment of gelignite destined for use at a local authority quarry at Soloheadbeg was about to be sent to the military barracks in Tipperary town. The explosives would then be taken by County Council employees under RIC escort to the quarry. The IRA estimated that the escort would consist of about six policemen. Volunteer Lar Breen, brother of Dan, gained employment at the quarry and provided intelligence to the brigade. Dan Breen and Treacy were on the run at the time and moved constantly around the county, staying in safe houses. A rudimentary headquarters for the ambush was established at a disused house on a farm at Greenane near Soloheadbeg, which became known as 'the tin hut'. Twelve members of the brigade were selected to participate in the ambush and from 15 January onwards two scouts were posted along the anticipated route each day to watch for the shipment. Another scout kept watch on the military barracks, with the intention of informing the ambush party the strength of the RIC escort, when it left and which of two potential routes, the Donohill or Boherkine roads, it would use. The remaining members of the ambush party concealed themselves nearby and lay in wait. The party spent each night in the tin hut. This routine was repeated over six consecutive days, but the consignment did not appear.

On the morning of 21 January the ambush party reassembled. Now reduced to eight in number because of the prolonged nature of the operation, it consisted of Robinson, Breen, Hogan, Treacy, Patrick O'Dwyer, Michael Ryan, Patrick McCormack and Tadhg Crowe. At about noon a scout signalled that a horse and cart containing the gelignite had left the barracks in Tipperary and was approaching. Two council employees, driver James Godfrey and his assistant Patrick Flynn, were on the cart. The police escort consisted of two RIC constables, James McDonnell and Patrick O'Connell, who walked behind the cart with carbines slung on their shoulders. Crowe later stated that they had been given instructions not to fire without orders from Treacy or Robinson.[21] O'Dwyer recalled that it was definitely the intention to hold up the escort, disarm them and 'seize the gelignite without bloodshed if possible'.[22] In later life Breen said that he and Treacy had decided before the ambush that they were going to shoot whatever number of police came along as an escort, but they did not tell Robinson of this plan.[23] The order 'hands up' was shouted by Treacy, but volleys of rifle and revolver shots rang out simultaneously and both constables were killed instantly.

O'Dwyer recalled that both council employees were very frightened, but Breen assured them that nothing was going to happen. O'Dwyer also stated that one of the council employees, James Godfrey, knew both Breen and Treacy well, and he believed that the other, Patrick Flynn, must have known them too.[24] The bodies of the dead policemen were searched, and their weapons, handcuffs and ammunition taken. Breen, Treacy and Hogan drove away in the horse and cart with the gelignite. Ryan and McCormack remained on the road with Robinson, guarding Godfrey and Flynn until such time as the gelignite was a safe distance away. Crowe and O'Dwyer later greased and carefully wrapped the carbines before hiding them in a field near Crowe's house. As the Crowe family was known to the RIC, the house and lands were searched on several occasions, but the police equipment was not discovered and it was subsequently passed to the brigade quartermaster. The gelignite captured during the ambush was divided among the various battalions of the Third Tipperary Brigade. As an old man, Breen expressed his regret that there had been only two policemen on the escort instead of the six that he expected, reasoning that 'six dead policemen would have impressed the country more than a mere two'.[25]

In the aftermath of the ambush, which was carried out against the express orders of IRA headquarters and led to the county being declared a special military area, Breen, Treacy and the others went on the run. The fact that the

Soloheadbeg ambush took place on the same day as the Dáil met in Dublin was coincidental, as the ambushers had lain in wait for six days. Nevertheless, for militants, this concurrence gave the ambush added symbolism. Adjutant Phil Fitzgerald of the Third Brigade believed that it 'set the heather on fire'.[26] While there had been sporadic attacks on the RIC since 1916, the Soloheadbeg ambush had a new element of ruthlessness that distinguished it from attacks of previous years. IRA Commander C. S. Andrews later expressed doubt, however, about Breen's claim that Soloheadbeg was a deliberately considered act, taken on his own initiative, to get the guerrilla campaign started, believing it instead to be an operation that had gone wrong, as elsewhere many policemen had 'been disarmed without being killed'.[27] The brutal nature of the ambush came as a shock to many moderate members of Sinn Féin and the Volunteer movement, as well as the wider population.

Constable O'Connell from Coachford in County Cork was thirty years old and engaged to be married. Constable McDonnell, a widower with seven children, was fifty-six and from Belmullet in County Mayo. He had served in Tipperary for over twenty-six years. Several days before the ambush he asked a friend in jest 'do you think the Sinn Féiners would shoot me? I don't think they would myself.'[28] An inquest into the deaths of the two constables took place on 22 January 1919. Council employees Godfrey and Flynn were called as witnesses and questioned by RIC District Inspector Browrigg as to the circumstances surrounding the ambush. The police believed that one or both of them knew the killers, but Inspector General Byrne reported that neither man could or would identify them.[29] Newspapers reported their evidence as being of the 'most confusing character' and Flynn fainted while in the witness box.[30] A poignant moment occurred during the inquest when the son of Constable McDonnell intervened and asked Godfrey whether his father had 'been given a dog's chance', and whether the policemen had been given time to hand over the explosives.[31] The coroner intervened to point out that the purpose of the inquest was only to ascertain the cause of death, but did express his opinion that both constables had been 'nailed on the spot'. He described the tragedy as one of the saddest cases that had happened in Tipperary or any part of Ireland for many years. He went on to say that he knew both policemen well and it was terribly sad to see them shot down while performing public duty and not doing anything that would injure anybody.[32] The jury returned a verdict that the deaths of the two policemen were due to shots fired by masked men, and added a rider expressing sympathy with their relatives.[33]

On 22 January public gatherings, including fairs and markets, were prohibited and 'Wanted' posters of Breen were posted outside every police barracks in the country, offering a reward of £1,000 for his capture. Descriptions of Treacy, Breen, Hogan and Robinson were published in *The Police Gazette*, also known as *Hue and Cry*. Shortly after the ambush, the murders were raised during parliamentary questions in the House of Lords by Tipperary landowner the Earl of Donoughmore. Seeking to clarify the amount of compensation to which their dependents might be entitled, Donoughmore referred to the policemen as victims of a brutal assassination, the perpetrators of which 'we are all very sorry to see no sign of finding'. He also expressed his desire that the government would see a way to deal generously with the issue of compensation. He added 'there is no question whatever that the spirit and loyalty to the public of the RIC is absolutely incontestable'. Because of the exceptional circumstances of the case, the treasury sanctioned the payment of a gratuity of £100 to the children of Constable McDonnell, and the payment of a compassionate grant of £25 to the parents of Constable O'Connell.

Several days after the ambush Commandant Jerome Davin of the Third Tipperary Brigade was in Rosegreen village and saw a police notice offering a substantial reward for information leading to the arrest and conviction of the IRA members responsible for the ambush. Davin replaced this poster with one of his own, threatening anyone who gave such information that they would meet a similar fate to the dead policemen. He signed the notice using the Latin term 'Veritas'. It was subsequently noticed by Tipperary Volunteers that when the police and military carried out house searches particular interest was shown in Latin textbooks, apparently searching for any reference to that particular word.[34]

Third Brigade Assistant Quartermaster Eamon O'Duibhir was imprisoned with other Volunteers in Durham Jail when the ambush took place. When news of Soloheadbeg reached them, opinion was divided among the prisoners as to whether it was the right or wrong course of action. Knowing the Tipperary men involved, O'Duibhir took their side but later recounted that the majority of the prisoners did not seem to think that it was a very good thing, which he believed reflected the feeling of the wider nationalist community. After being released from jail, he found a great deal of ill-feeling against the men who had taken part in this attack, and that local newspapers had strongly condemned the ambush.

O'Duibhir wrote to the *Tipperary Star* newspaper stating that while nobody liked to see men killed, the RIC were holding the country down for England and 'it was regrettable but the men who did the firing could not be blamed ... they were serving the Irish nation and fighting for its independence'.[35] Others disagreed, however, and during the Requiem Mass for Constable McDonnell at St Michael's church in Tipperary town, Monsignor Ryan read out a letter from Dr Harty, Archbishop of the Diocese of Cashel and Emly. Condemning the killings as cold-blooded murder for which there was no justification, Harty remarked, 'it used to be remarked that where Tipperary leads, Ireland follows ... but God help poor Ireland if she follows this deed of blood'.[36]

The Soloheadbeg ambush was carried out in contravention of instructions that had been issued by IRA Chief of Staff Richard Mulcahy, thus causing tension between GHQ and those who carried it out. In later life Mulcahy wrote that he 'frequently despaired' of Tipperary Volunteers as they rejected his efforts at imposing military discipline on them.[37] He also believed that, as the ambush had been taken entirely on the initiative of Tipperary Volunteers, it could not be endorsed by the IRA leadership and if they were captured or killed by the police, it could not be acknowledged that they had acted with authority; they would be branded as 'common murderers'.[38] Mulcahy ordered Robinson, Breen, Hogan and Treacy to leave Ireland and go to America, but they refused. Following an intervention by Michael Collins, 'the big four' went instead to Dublin and joined a group of IRA Volunteers colloquially known as 'the squad'. These men were recruited by Collins to carry out assassinations of key military, political and police personnel. Mulcahy believed that, insofar as the

Tipperary men were concerned, 'their services were not required and their presence was often awkward' in Dublin.[39] Collins, however, believed that Ireland would benefit more from conflict and a state of disorder 'than from a continuation of the situation as it now stands'.[40]

Shortly after the ambush, officers of the Third Tipperary Brigade issued a declaration, signed by Séamus Robinson, which threatened soldiers and policemen that if they did not leave the county, they would 'forfeit their lives'.[41] GHQ refused to sanction the proclamation, adding to the existing tension. Within the brigade itself, there was division and animosity in later years about the reality of Soloheadbeg. In 1950 Séamus Robinson refused an invitation to attend the unveiling of a memorial at the site of the ambush. He was heavily critical of the version of events contained in Breen's autobiography and cited his belief that, despite being the officer in command of the Third Tipperary Brigade and a veteran of the 1916 Rising, his part in the ambush had been minimised.[42]

After the Soloheadbeg ambush, many Volunteers believed that the police became more aggressive, and those suspected of involvement frequently had their houses raided. For many Volunteers, however, the increased activity on the part of the RIC only had the effect of inspiring more action.[43] IRA member Michael Fitzpatrick recalled that many Volunteers were taken by surprise at events and took some time to recover from the shock caused by the shootings. He believed, however, that Treacy was a 'true prophet', and that the raids and greater police attention that ensued served only to raise the morale of officers and men. He recalled that even those who had been shocked after the ambush became active in the movement again. Prisons rapidly filled with Volunteers arrested for drilling and other activities, and Tipperary men 'were to the fore again'.[44]

Reporting on the Soloheadbeg ambush, *The Manchester Guardian* editorialised that English people would misunderstand the situation entirely if they thought that 'such casual and cold blooded murders formed any part of official Sinn Féin policy ... on the contrary, they are utterly repudiated and detested in Harcourt Street' (the location of Sinn Féin's headquarters).[45] The *Daily News* reported on the wider significance of the killings and what might result from them, stating that 'well-meaning idealists in Dáil Éireann were utterly unable to control the physical-force men in the provinces'. It further reported that Dáil Éireann was less important than it looked, having 'the appearance of power while the reality lies in the hands of men who believe that the salvation of Ireland is to be found in gelignite and revolvers.[46] The ambush also caused profound shock within the RIC and was viewed as an ominous escalation in the recent pattern of attacks on the police. Patrick Shea, the son of an RIC sergeant serving in Tipperary, recalled that in the barracks where the family lived there was 'incredulity, fear, horror, and angry words.' The dead constables were known to most policemen in the county and there was nervous speculation about what the future might hold. Shea's father was 'silent and grim ... mother could not conceal her anxiety'. Even though Shea was only eleven at the time, he realised that his father's profession was dangerous, and if his father was late coming home the family lay awake and listened for the sound of his step. 'Father became the centre of our thoughts and we were frightened and sorry for him.'[47]

Inspector General Byrne of the RIC reported that there had been no improvement in the attitude of the people towards the police who, in the more disaffected counties, were treated with bitter hostility and boycotted in various ways. He stated that this was to undermine their loyalty and sow discontent by making it appear that their loyalty to duty was condemned by nationalist opinion as unpatriotic. Byrne did not seem to realise the gravity of the situation, however, commenting that intelligence in his possession did not amount to definite information that an outbreak of conflict would actually take place. He did acknowledge that a state of dangerous unrest existed, to which he felt 'bound to invite the attention of Government'.[48] The situation escalated dramatically on 31 January 1919 when *An t-Óglách* ominously declared a state of war to exist between Ireland and England: 'Every Volunteer is entitled to use all legitimate methods of warfare against the soldiers and policemen of the English usurper and to slay them if necessary.'[49] Byrne dismissed *An t-Óglách* as 'pernicious material' carrying instructions for demolishing railways and bridges, but the implications of this declaration were clear. The IRA had declared war on the British Empire, and their fellow Irishmen in the RIC were identified as the main target of their campaign.

In March 1919 Byrne reported his concern at the tone of speeches given by recently elected Sinn Féin members of parliament, which showed an increasing hostility towards the RIC. One such speech was given by Séamus Bourke, Sinn Féin TD for mid-Tipperary, who said that the correct way to deal with the police was not to shoot them, as it would be inexpedient, 'but to make their life unbearable, treat them as outcasts of society, as we cannot be in any place that some of these vipers are not in our midst'. Byrne commented that inflammatory speeches were 'indicative of an intention to make governance impossible by intimidation of the police'. He concluded by saying that Ireland was unquestionably in a highly inflammable condition and, in his opinion, at no time was there more urgent necessity for the presence of an overpowering military force'.[50]

A significant escalation in the campaign against the RIC occurred on 10 April 1920, when the Dáil formally authorised a boycott of the police. This policy had been followed by Volunteers at a local level for the previous two years, and the formalisation of the strategy became the basis for the campaign of the IRA thereafter. The resolution, moved by Éamon de Valera, called on Irish people to ostracise members of the police publicly and socially.[51] Eoin MacNeill, founder of the Irish Volunteers, seconded the motion, opining that the police in Ireland was a force of traitors.[52] A definition of 'social ostracisation' was presented to the Dáil, which declared that the police should be treated as if they were guilty of treason, unworthy to enjoy any of the privileges or comforts that arise from cordial relations with the public.[53] It went on to stipulate that policemen and their families should receive no social recognition from the people except such as was absolutely necessary and that they should not be saluted, spoken to or their greetings returned. It stated that they should not be invited to or received in houses as friends or guests, that they should be barred from participation in games, sports, dances and all social functions, and 'that intermarriage with them be discouraged'.[54] A fortnight later, on 26 April 1919, the executive committee of Cumann na mBan instructed its members not to be in company with nor speak to a policeman, or even occupy the same bench as one in church.[55] To accompany these declarations a document under the title 'Aceldama', a biblical term for a place associated with slaughter and bloodshed, was circulated with the instruction that it should be copied four times and sent to four additional people.[56]

> For money their hands are dipped in the blood of their people
> They are the eyes and ears of the enemy
> Let those eyes and ears know no friendship
> Let them be outcasts in their own land
> The blood of the martyrs shall be on them and their children's children, and they shall curse the mothers that bring them forth.[57]

Addressing the Dáil in April 1919, Éamon de Valera described the RIC as 'spies in our midst' and went on to say that they should not be tolerated socially as if they were law-abiding citizens; they should be made to understand that 'the people of Ireland loathed them and their vocation'.[58] Inspector General Byrne reported extensively on the significant increase in the number of public meetings, concerts and lectures attended by Sinn Féin politicians 'in pursuance of the policy to undermine and corrupt the loyalty of the force'. He referred to a speech given on 20 April 1919, during which Sinn Féin MP for Cork North Patrick O'Keefe referred to the RIC as a 'black army', alleging that if it was not for that force, Ireland would have its freedom. He urged parents with sons in the police to write and ask them 'for God's sake to come home ... they are decent fathers' and mothers' sons but the moment they go inside the gate of that depot they are completely changed'. Byrne believed that organised hostility to the police, besides endangering their lives, was part of the scheme to 'make British government in Ireland impossible'.[59]

A significant sequel to the Soloheadbeg ambush occurred on 13 May 1919 when Seán Hogan was arrested while attending a dance at the house of Eamon O'Duibhir. Breen and Treacy formulated an audacious plan to rescue him while he was being moved from Thurles RIC barracks to jail in Cork city, the usual destination for prisoners arrested under the Defence of the Realm Act. Hogan was escorted by four policemen, including arresting officer Sergeant Peter Wallace and Constable Michael Enright. When the train stopped at Knocklong railway station, Wallace reportedly taunted Hogan with the remark 'where are Breen and Treacy now?'[60] At that moment several IRA members, including Breen and Treacy, boarded the train and fired a number of shots at the police escort, which resulted in the deaths of Wallace and Enright. Despite being seriously injured in the exchange of fire, Breen and Treacy managed to rescue Hogan, and both men subsequently recovered from their wounds.

Treacy later received a message from Michael Collins that congratulated him on a 'magnificent achievement'. Breen recollected that, for IRA Volunteers, such praise from Collins was comparable to the 'awarding of a Victoria Cross to a British soldier'.[61] Reporting the incident, Inspector General Byrne stated that local people had been 'perfectly callous' and gave no assistance to the police in tracing the men responsible. In Thurles the slogans 'Knocklong Aboo', 'Up Knocklong' and 'Wallace bowled over, RIP' were written on a road, and the widow of Sergeant Wallace was heckled while on her way to Mass.[62] IRA Volunteer Michael Davern reminisced that when he informed Breen's mother about Knocklong, the injuries to her son and that two members of the RIC had died her reply was 'Christ, isn't it a pity that they did not kill all four of the bastards.'[63] After a trial at Armagh Crown Court on 9 March 1920, three men were found guilty of the killings at Knocklong. Edmund Foley and Patrick Maher were executed in Dublin on 7 June 1921.[64] The third man, Michael Murphy, was imprisoned but released shortly after the Truce in July 1921. Foley and Maher had only peripheral roles in the ambush, and are not named on the official memorial to the rescue, which is located at the old Knocklong railway station.

Following the Knocklong incident, Tipperary remained designated as a special military area. Byrne stated that the police were regarded by the extremists as the great obstacle to the realisation of their political aims, and also expressed his opinion that the most effective means of preventing further similar incidents was the retention of a powerful military force in Ireland. Increased activity and tactics employed by the police as hostilities escalated were viewed by many IRA members as being beneficial to their cause. Séamus Babington, engineering officer of the Third Tipperary Brigade, believed that if the deaths of RIC men had been used by the police as propaganda instead of engaging in 'manhunts and the wholesale raiding and opening up of the floodgates of fury it was possible the spirit of Republicanism would not have rekindled'.[65] He also felt that, insofar as IRA Volunteers were concerned, 'police hostile action, ruthless treatment of the civil population and their unbridled hatred of any suspects or genuine republicanism and nationalism ... their open tyranny was a Godsend'.[66]

There is general consensus among historians that the Soloheadbeg ambush was the key incident that triggered the

1919–21 conflict, which has been variously described as the Anglo-Irish War, the War of Independence, the Black and Tan war or the Irish Revolution. The fact that two long-serving policemen were killed on the same day as the Dáil met for the first time was seen by many militant Volunteers as the physical embodiment of an aspiration expressed by that Dáil to achieve Irish independence. Cathal Brugha believed that Volunteers should only be used to influence the outcome of events, and not actually to fight, whereas others, such as IRA Chief of Staff Richard Mulcahy, believed that they would have a more active role in the forthcoming conflict, describing them as 'an armed military force ... which would defend the growth of the parliament and secure and maintain its prestige and authority'.[67]

Tensions heightened significantly on 23 June 1919 when, in front of a large crowd returning from a race meeting in Thurles, District Inspector Michael Hunt was shot dead in Liberty Square. Hunt and his colleague District Inspector Wilson from the adjacent Templemore RIC district had been particularly active against the Volunteer movement for several years. In March 1918 they had both been involved in a mass arrest of local Volunteers, including Commandant Seán Gaynor of the First Tipperary Brigade, who later recalled being 'hauled out of bed at 4 a.m. by a large force of police under Hunt and Wilson'.[68] In the weeks leading up to his death, Hunt had broken up several Sinn Féin meetings, for which he had received a first-class commendation.[69] Commandant Patrick Kinnane of the Second Brigade recalled that much concern had been caused to brigade and battalion officers by the 'villainy of Hunt and his unscrupulous and ruthless tactics'.[70] Following the arrest by Hunt of IRA Vice

Commandant Michael 'Mixey' O'Connell in Thurles in connection with the Knocklong killings, Commandant James Leahy of the Second Tipperary Brigade discussed with other brigade members the proposal that Hunt should be killed. It was believed that, if Hunt continued to operate with impunity, it could have disastrous results and that his shooting 'would have a salutary effect on other policemen who might be inclined to follow his example'.[71] Commandant Jerry Ryan stated that Hunt was specifically targeted because of raids and searches in which he had been involved, when he had 'made himself most obnoxious to the people because of the brutal manner in which he carried them out'.[72] Hunt had also been involved in the arrest of Sinn Féin MP Ernest Blythe in May 1919 at Inchivella near Thurles, for being in possession of seditious documents while addressing a meeting. The documents contained instructions as to how the RIC boycott should be carried out and their morale damaged. An extract from the documents given during Blythe's subsequent trial concluded that an energetic 'bad lad' of a peeler could be made quiet if it were discovered where he was from and word sent to local Volunteers or Sinn Féiners, with a view to making things 'unpleasant for his people who will not fail to inform him of how they suffer for his activity'.[73]

Plans were made to assassinate Hunt while he was on duty at a race meeting, but a suitable opportunity to do so did not arise at the racecourse. As he returned to the RIC barracks in town with the rest of the RIC party, he was shot three times at close range by 'Big Jim' Stapleton who, along with several other IRA Volunteers, had mingled with the large crowd returning from the races. The crowd initially panicked and fled in all directions, allowing the killers to escape without difficulty. As Hunt lay dying on the roadway a considerable crowd collected about 'jeering and laughing but did not assist'.[74] Leahy stated that for some hours after the shooting the police appeared to be nervous, but as the evening wore on they got intoxicated, and demonstrated their fury by 'beating up anyone who they could get their hands on, especially Sinn Féin supporters'. Later that night Leahy was in O'Connell's bar in Thurles when an RIC head constable whom he knew came into the bar. Leahy recalled that the policeman was a 'good sort and advanced in years, and had no interest in the actions of his colleagues outside on the streets, nor did he approve of them'.[75] When offered a glass of whiskey by Leahy, the policeman readily accepted. Leahy took this to mean the IRA had correctly anticipated the police's response to Hunt's shooting.

At the inquest, which took place in Richmond Barracks in Templemore the day after the killing, the jury returned a verdict of 'wilful murder by a person or persons unknown'.[76] County Inspector Mulliner reported that this verdict had only been reached after considerable hesitation and a grudging expression of sympathy to the relatives of the deceased made by the jurors. Mulliner linked the death of Hunt to the previous RIC deaths at Soloheadbeg and Knocklong, which he described as the 'first blows', and also to the recent arrest by Hunt of O'Donnell, which had incurred 'bitter hostility' in the locality.[77] Hunt left behind a wife and five children. Archbishop Harty condemned his murder as a flagrant violation of the fifth commandment.[78] But, he also strongly criticised the provocative action of the government and gave his opinion that the military domination of Ireland should cease at once.[79]

Notwithstanding the killing of Hunt, the restrictions of the Defence of the Realm Act, which had been imposed after the Soloheadbeg ambush, were lifted on 14 June. On 26 June, however, the Lord Lieutenant John French sent a telegram to the government in London stating his belief that Sinn Féin was 'an organised club for the murder of police'. He went on to demand that Sinn Féin in Tipperary should be proclaimed an illegal organisation. While there was sporadic IRA activity throughout Ireland, the inspector general identified Munster as the most difficult province to police. It was necessary for the military to assist the police with most of their duties, particularly when duties of what he termed a 'political nature' had to be performed. Byrne reported the belief of IRA members that, because their self-declared Irish Republic was at war with the British Empire, they were fully justified in killing policemen. He described it as an 'absurd doctrine ... but evidently one that is accepted by many of these fanatical young men'. Byrne also referred to an incident in which an RIC sergeant had been warned by a priest that there was 'a class of men going about who think it is no sin to shoot a policeman because they say that they are at war with England ... no policeman's life is safe at present.'[80]

A week after Lord Lieutenant French's request a proclamation under the Criminal Law and Procedure (Ireland) Act was issued. This suppressed all Sinn Féin organisations in Tipperary as well as the Gaelic League, Cumann na mBan and the Irish Volunteers.[81] Byrne reported that the proclamation was 'received with indifference by the inhabitants' who appeared relieved that further restrictions on fairs and markets had not been imposed.[82] Additional police and troops were drafted into the county, which had a temporary calming effect. A key factor for the relatively quiet state of Tipperary following the dramatic events in Soloheadbeg, Knocklong and Thurles was the absence from the county of some of its most violent activists. Breen and Hogan had been badly wounded during the Knocklong ambush and spent time recuperating in Kerry. Treacy and Robinson went to Dublin and by the late summer of 1919 Breen and Hogan had also joined them in the city at the request of Michael Collins. Collins admired 'men of action', so the Tipperary Volunteers were 'taken under his wing ... with the combination of his brains and their brawn proving to be ... lethal'.[83]

Breen and Hogan would not return to Tipperary until 1920, having first taken part in an audacious assassination attempt on Lord Lieutenant French near his Phoenix Park lodge on 19 December 1919. Collins had arranged that the Tipperary men would assist the members of the Dublin Brigade in this attack. It was believed that if French were killed 'his death would arouse all peoples to take notice of our fight for freedom'.[84] Reporting this 'dastardly attempt' on the life of French, the RIC inspector general referred to the 'these seditious and truculent Volunteers', saying that they had 'sufficient arms and explosives hidden away for committing outrages, or guerilla warfare as they call it'. He also reported that at a recent meeting of the Dáil, the taking of an oath of allegiance to the Irish Republic was made incumbent on all members and on all IRA Volunteers. The oath included the words 'I will support and defend the Irish Republic, and the government of the Irish Republic, which is Dáil Éireann, against all enemies, foreign and domestic ... so help me God'.[85] It was obvious that, insofar as the IRA was concerned, members of the RIC were the 'domestic enemies' in question.

To accurately record escalating lawlessness, a new category entitled 'Outrages against the Police' was added to the existing comprehensive monthly reports submitted by each district and county inspector to the RIC inspector general. These detailed attacks not only on RIC members and police stations, but also incidents of intimidation, boycotting and threats towards barrack servants, merchants and suppliers, landlords, RIC applicants and pensioners.[86] Also included in these reports were cases of local women who had their heads 'bobbed' or forcibly shaved as a public humiliation for what was termed 'keeping company with policemen'.[87] The provinces of Munster and Connacht were regularly cited as being particularly hostile to the police. Byrne said that the IRA was 'committed in pursuance of a deliberate campaign to break the morale of the police, which is often referred to as the last obstacle in the way of an Irish Republic'.[88]

In Tipperary, the brief lull in hostilities that took place following the killing of District Inspector Hunt ended violently on 2 September 1919 when another policeman met his death. IRA Volunteers from the Lorrha area planned an ambush on an RIC patrol, but a dispute with IRA headquarters was ongoing. The Lorrha company had been placed in the Birr battalion area as part of the Second Offaly Brigade, but as Tipperary men the Volunteers wanted to be under the control of the First Tipperary Brigade. Breen and Treacy were asked to use their influence with GHQ to have the battalion transferred, and Breen undertook to assist. He also sent word that the ambush should take place, informing the Volunteers that he had received sanction for it from headquarters. Despite their absence from Tipperary, the influence of 'the big four' continued to be felt.

The police patrol in question took place on a nightly basis, when one sergeant and two constables from Lorrha Barracks patrolled from Lorrha village towards the townland of Carrigahorig. Seven IRA Volunteers were armed with an assortment of revolvers and shotguns, but very little ammunition. The RIC patrol left their barracks at 9 p.m. and it was decided to attack them as they returned around ninety minutes later. The ambushers lay in wait behind a wall and as the patrol cycled past, the command 'Hands up!' was given, accompanied by gunfire. Sergeant Brady and Constable Foley were badly wounded in the initial fusillade, with Brady calling out 'My God, I am shot,' before collapsing on the roadway, where he died shortly afterwards. Brady was forty-six and married with six children. He had arrived in Lorrha only two days before the ambush, having been previously stationed in Enniskillen. Constable McCormack managed to find cover and return fire on their attackers. Volunteer Martin Needham recalled that the accurate shooting of the policeman sent 'bullets uncomfortably close' to the Volunteers, forcing them to retreat.

In the aftermath of the ambush, extensive searches took place and the police questioned all known local Volunteers, including most of the ambush party. After being identified by Constable Foley as one of the gunmen, John Madden was subsequently charged with the murder of Sergeant Brady. Other Volunteers believed that Madden was charged because he was the 'talkative and boastful type, and not the class of man who could be trusted'. Following the ambush, Father Gleeson, the parish priest of Lorrha, strongly condemned it from the pulpit, denouncing the killers as criminals.[89] He stated that the 'brand of Cain lay upon the assassins ... the shadow of the crime would hang over the parish for many generations'.[90] This denunciation caused concern to some of the Volunteers involved as they were 'devout Catholics ... attentive to their religious duties'.[91] Needham then approached a priest in the nearby town of Portumna in County Galway who was more sympathetic to the Volunteer cause. This priest subsequently heard confessions and gave absolution to all of the men who had been involved in the ambush. Following his condemnation of the killing, it was reported that Father Gleeson received abusive and threatening letters. It was further reported that a series of threatening notices were placed in the area directed 'at the police or those that have shown any friendly disposition towards the police'. On 15 September 1919, for example, a horse was shot dead and the local police believed it was because the owner had delivered turf to Lorrha Barracks.[92]

Those involved in the Lorrha ambush received a severe reprimand from the senior officers of the Second Offaly Brigade as, contrary to what Breen had told Needham and others prior to the ambush, it had not been authorised by GHQ. The maintenance of military discipline within the ranks of the IRA was a serious issue for GHQ and local commanders at that time, as many attacks were being carried out by local units without the advance approval of brigade staff.[93] Sinn Féin had been suppressed in Tipperary following the killing of District Inspector Hunt; following the death of Sergeant Brady, public assemblies, including fairs and markets, were also prohibited. County Inspector Mulliner reported that this prohibition was received with 'dismay as it directly affected the local population, particularly in financial terms'. Despite the reprimand from GHQ, the Lorrha company was subsequently transferred into the First Tipperary Brigade area at the request of Breen, becoming part of the fourth battalion of that brigade.

On 7 September 1919, a notice was posted near Rearcross Barracks stating that those associating with the police would forfeit their lives, and that animals and vehicles placed at the disposal of the police would be destroyed. Describing this incident, the Lorrha ambush and other similar incidents that were taking place throughout Ireland, the inspector general stated that they were 'eloquent of the difficulties and danger with which the constabulary has to contend in the discharge of their duties'.[94] When the conflict initially erupted in Tipperary, attacks carried out against the RIC were disorganised and primarily opportunist in nature. Gradually, however, as the IRA became more organised and effective as a fighting force, a systematic guerrilla campaign developed. The tactic of combining physical violence with intimidation and ostracisation proved to be hugely effective and quickly spread throughout the country, albeit to greater effect in counties such as Tipperary, Cork and Clare.

As 1919 drew to a close the British government struggled to define the disparate roles of the police and army in the conflict, apparently unwilling to concede that Ireland was in a state of rebellion and that, in many counties, the King's writ had effectively ceased to function. Prime Minister Lloyd George stated that counter-insurgency was a job for the police supported by the military and not vice versa. He also made the assertion that 'war could not be declared on rebels'.[95] The inspector general requested the deployment of a substantial number of additional troops to Ireland as Sinn Féiners were 'saturated with hostility to British rule and should they receive a general order to give trouble it would no doubt be obeyed, the police would be overwhelmingly outnumbered and the situation would necessitate strong military action'.[96] Again, he singled out the province of Munster where 'the spirit of lawlessness was particularly manifest ... and where the police would not be strong enough to cope with it but for the assistance afforded by the military'.[97]

The government decided that a change of leadership within the RIC was required, so Inspector General Byrne was first placed on leave and then replaced by his deputy, Thomas J. Smyth. The RIC had a byzantine structure, which left it ill-prepared for the situation that had arisen, and Byrne had resisted suggestions that ex-servicemen should be recruited into the RIC to bolster the force. Prime Minister Lloyd George already believed that war could not be declared on rebels, and told the cabinet that the 'Irish job would fail if it became a military job only'.[98] The Irish garrison could not provide the number of troops needed to assist the police, who were finding it increasingly difficult to cope with a full-scale guerrilla campaign. Lloyd George believed that Byrne should be replaced by a man of 'less intelligence and stolidity' as head of the RIC.[99] Religious considerations may also have played a part in Byrne's removal, as he had been the first Roman Catholic to hold the position of inspector general. He had failed to hold the confidence of the powerful figure Walter Long, chairman of the cabinet committee given the mandate of arriving at a settlement to the Irish problem, who said that having a Catholic at the head of the RIC had 'caused a leakage in high quarters which has led to the defeat of justice'.[100]

On 25 November 1919 the prohibition order under the Criminal Law and Procedure (Ireland) Act, which had hitherto suppressed nationalist organisations in only certain counties, was extended to all of Ireland. As Christmas approached the practice ceased, in what were categorised as the 'more disturbed areas', of having isolated RIC barracks and police huts in rural settings manned by three or four policemen. Constables were instead moved to larger barracks that were easier to fortify. This had the effect of adding physical isolation to the growing estrangement of the police from the population they served.[101] The *Constabulary Gazette* printed an editorial that reflected the frustration of many rank-and-file members of the force:

> Why wear uniform? Why proceed on patrol according to red tape? Why continue to occupy ridiculous little arsenals in sparsely populated districts? Why pursue the old methods, now obviously clumsy and obsolete? The men who shoot the police are very clever, of this there is no room for doubt.[102]

As 1919 ended, the men of the constabulary throughout Ireland reflected on what had been a harrowing year. War had been declared on the force by the IRA, and fifteen policemen had been killed. Intimidation and ostracisation were rife, and large swathes of the country were left without a visible police presence as the RIC retreated to fortified barracks in larger towns. Ireland was on a knife-edge, and members of the constabulary faced a dangerous and uncertain future.

Tipperary was a violent county within a particularly violent province. While Munster contained only a quarter of the population of Ireland, it consistently accounted for more than half of the attributable police casualties every year from

1919 until the end of the conflict in 1921.[103] Geography and topography were of fundamental importance in the IRA campaign. Military intelligence reports for the sixth division area, headquartered in Limerick and responsible for Tipperary, referred to the vast number of sparsely populated mountain districts and the extensive expanses of uninhabited bogs, which gave a certain immunity to roving guerrilla bands, 'while the numerous banks, hedges and sunken roads afford nearly every route with an ideal site for an ambush on the military'.[104]

The RIC was now firmly on the front line against an increasingly powerful and emboldened IRA. Inspector General Smyth continued the policy of evacuating isolated RIC barracks and temporary posts. This measure enabled the augmentation of the barracks that remained open, and allowed patrols to be strengthened. Smyth signalled that while this policy was necessary for operational reasons, it had caused apprehension among law-abiding citizens in the abandoned districts, who felt that they were being left without adequate protection.[105] Smyth cited Munster as being particularly afflicted with a 'sprit of lawlessness', and admitted that, but for the assistance of the military, the RIC would not be strong enough to cope.

If the RIC could no longer police an area, its very existence was in doubt. The ruthlessness and determination of the IRA exposed the deficiencies of the RIC as a civil police force. Limerick-based District Inspector John Regan found that many policemen under his command were only suited from a 'gendarmerie point of view to deal with a few armed moonlighters ... dealing with organised bodies of violent men was completely out of the class of most of them'.[106] Large expanses of Ireland were now effectively under the control of the IRA. The danger of this development was highlighted by the inspector general, who held that if country districts could be constantly traversed at night by strong patrols, bodies of IRA Volunteers could be detected and dealt with. With limited numbers, however, the RIC could do little more than defend their barracks.[107] Even this was proving to be increasingly difficult and on 8 November 1919 an order was issued that as many barracks as necessary should be closed to ensure that the remaining barracks had a station party of at least six men each.[108] Byrne also informed the government that control of the nationalist movement had passed to the 'extreme section, who may now be regarded as an oath-bound society scarcely indistinguishable from the Irish Republican Brotherhood'.[109] In January 1920 IRA headquarters devolved authority to local brigade commanders to carry out attacks in their respective areas without prior sanction. Prior to this, some Volunteers had carried out attacks, such as the Lorrha ambush, on their own initiative, which had resulted in the deaths of Volunteers or had caused larger operations to be abandoned. There was concern within the IRA that a Volunteer 'wishing to make a name for himself, might shoot a friendly member of the enemy forces who was doing useful work for our intelligence people'.[110]

Events in Dublin during January 1920 had major consequences for the evolving conflict throughout Ireland. On 21 January the IRA struck a major blow against the already weakened G Division of the DMP. G Division was quite small, with about twenty detectives, and aside from political policing, it also carried out investigations into ordinary crime and was responsible for the licensing of carriages. Several detectives were killed following their refusal to resign as the IRA had demanded in threatening letters. Three of the remaining detectives, David Nelligan, Ned Broy and James McNamara, were actually working for Michael Collins, supplying information on the activities of other members of the division. In an effort to restore its effectiveness, RIC Inspector William Redmond from Belfast was appointed as assistant commissioner of the DMP, and assigned the role of reorganising G Division. He was immediately recognised as a serious threat by Collins, who observed 'if we don't get that man he will get us, and soon'.[111] On 21 January 1920 Redmond was shot dead as he made his way from Dublin Castle to the Standard Hotel in Harcourt Street. On 14 April 1920 Detective Constable Henry Kells was killed on Camden Street, and on 20 April 1920 Detective Constable Laurence Dalton was shot dead at Broadstone. These killings brought about the end of G Division's reign as potent adversaries of the IRA.[112] Dublin Castle offered a reward of £10,000 for information leading to convictions in the five murders of G Division detectives and in nine murders of RIC members. A reward of £1,000 was also offered for 'secret information which would assist the police'.[113]

Early in January 1920 members of the Second Tipperary Brigade met in Thurles to plan a new series of attacks. There were eighteen police barracks in their brigade area and it was agreed to attack several simultaneously in an IRA show of strength. Such attacks also served to sap the morale of policemen, as it was believed that shots fired at their strongholds 'had a nuisance value ... well worthwhile for the few rounds of ammunition expended'. The date chosen was 18 January. Police barracks at Holycross and Drombane were attacked by ambush parties, while those at

Barnane, Borrisoleigh, Roskeen and Templetouhy were shot at by snipers. The attacks had the desired effect, and the IRA watched policemen inside the barracks who 'spent the whole night recklessly firing their rifles at imaginary attackers'.[114] In the course of the Drombane attack, the IRA captured three policemen who were returning from patrol, holding them hostage for the duration of the attack. They were later released, after being disarmed.

Less fortunate was Constable Luke Finnegan, stationed in Thurles. Having been responsible for the distribution of the sugar ration during the First World War, he had extensive local knowledge and was very familiar with local Volunteers. More significantly, Finnegan was an important witness in the case against IRA Volunteers involved in the Knocklong rescue, which was believed by the county inspector to be the reason he was singled out to be killed.[115] Commandant Jimmy Leahy believed that Finnegan was 'very hostile to the Republican movement and was known to have been busy making inquiries into the activities of IRA members'. Just after the barracks attacks of 18 January, Finnegan told Leahy that the RIC knew who had been involved and that they would be 'rounded up shortly'. Leahy, however, was also receiving information from a police sergeant in Thurles who was on friendly terms with some local Volunteers, and he provided information that Finnegan was in the process of compiling a list of IRA suspects for the attacks. It was then decided that Finnegan should be killed.[116]

On the night of 20 January, Leahy, Jerry Ryan, Michael Small and John McCarthy waited for Finnegan near his house at The Mall, Thurles, armed with revolvers. As Finnegan returned home from the police barracks, he was shot just yards from his home. He was hit three times and badly wounded, but managed to reach home before collapsing in front of his wife. Newspapers reported that he said 'Mary, I am done, what will you and the little babies do?'[117] Finnegan was treated by a local doctor before being removed to Dublin, where he was operated on at Doctor Steevens' Hospital, but subsequently died of his wounds.[118] At the inquest, which took place two days later in Dublin, the jury returned a verdict of 'wilful murder' and went on to condemn the killing as a 'dastardly outrage ... one of those wicked murders which are unfortunately disgracing the country at present'.[119]

A Thurles woman who had gone to the assistance of Finnegan subsequently received a letter threatening her with death, and a shopkeeper who had supplied goods to the police in the town received similar correspondence.[120] Several days after Finnegan's death, Sinn Féin supporters in the town awoke to find the letters 'RIP' painted on their houses. This act was later characterised by the local IRA leadership as 'an act of vandalism, rather than a portent of murderous consequences'.[121] Finnegan's death led to a much more significant shift in the pattern of conflict when a reprisal, which became known as the 'sack of Thurles', was carried out by the military and the police. Inhabitants were described as being in a 'state of utmost terror for several hours' as shots were fired and windows smashed by the RIC and by soldiers of the Sherwood Foresters garrisoned in the town.[122] The offices of the *Tipperary Star* newspaper were damaged by grenades and rifle fire. County Inspector Davin reported these incidents to Dublin Castle, admitting that 'the police wrecked fourteen houses in Thurles, the property or residences of prominent Sinn Féiners'.[123]

Mark Sturgis, Assistant Under-Secretary at Dublin Castle, wrote in his diary that in some cases senior RIC officers had given tacit approval to such attacks, and he noted a meeting with a district inspector in Tipperary whom he referred to as a 'professional reprisaler'. Sturgis believed that the rationale behind the police reprisal was to have 'the local blackguards marked – they know it and they know that they will personally pay the price if a policeman is shot'.[124] Responding to criticism of such retaliations, Lloyd George wrote in the *Daily Chronicle* that 'nobody can fail to deplore such occurrences but equally obviously nobody can wonder at them'. He went on to say that if the campaign against the police continued by what he described as 'murderous clubs, counter clubs may spring up and the lives of prominent Sinn Féiners could become as unsafe as prominent officials'.[125]

The cycle of reprisal and counter-reprisal continued. IRA Volunteers were branded as thugs and murderers by the government, and in turn the police and military were given the same label by insurgents.[126] The movements of troops and police were constantly watched by the IRA, with a view to opportunities and locations for ambushes. In March 1920 IRA Volunteers planned an attack on a joint patrol of military and RIC officers in Thurles. It had been noticed by IRA scouts that patrols regularly stopped at the market house in the centre of the town for breaks during lengthy periods of night duty. An ambush was planned for the night of 4 March. Numerous narrow laneways adjacent to the market house provided cover for the ambush and also escape routes. More than twenty-five Volunteers were scheduled to take part in the attack, but events elsewhere necessitated the abandonment of the ambush.

While on their way to take part in the attack, Jim Stapleton, Jim Larkin and Pat O'Brien called to Fanning's public house at The Ragg, Bouladuff, near Thurles, for a drink. While they were in the bar two uniformed RIC constables, John Heanue and John O'Flaherty from Dovea Barracks, entered the bar. The Volunteers decided on the spur of the moment to attack the policemen, and opened fire with revolvers.[127] There was an exchange of shots, during which O'Flaherty managed to escape, but Heanue was badly wounded and died the following day at the military hospital in Tipperary town. When news of the shooting reached the IRA in Thurles, Commandant Jimmy Leahy knew that 'it had upset my plans for the attack on the night patrol, and obliged me to abandon it'.

At the inquest into Heanue's death some days later, publican Laurence Fanning gave a graphic account of the incident. He stated that three men were at the bar drinking when the two policeman entered and ordered drinks. After a short interval the civilians rushed from their places and the command 'Hands up!' was shouted, but Constable Heanue opened fire, which was returned. O'Flaherty also fired on the IRA men who, following an exchange of shots, retreated. Fanning deposed that eight shots were fired in total, one of which had hit Heanue and caused his fatal injury.

The shooting led to a number of raids and reprisals by the police and military in the vicinity. On 4 March local IRA Volunteers James McCarthy and Tom Dwyer were shot dead in their homes by masked men, and the IRA claimed that the culprits were policemen in disguise. Dwyer had been questioned by the RIC following the shooting at The Ragg, as he had been seen talking to the three men in the pub prior to the incident. Dwyer was warned by his comrades to go on the run, but he had refused to do so. Following the two deaths, Tipperary Volunteer Edward McGrath was sent to Cork city to try and identify a specific policeman who the IRA believed had been involved in the shooting of Dwyer. McGrath spent several days watching police patrols at their assembly point, but when he did not see the policeman he was looking for, he returned to Tipperary.[128]

When reprisals began, it was initially well-known Sinn Féin members and their supporters who were targeted, but as the conflict intensified, attacks became more indiscriminate. Soldiers and policemen increasingly found it difficult to distinguish friend from foe and reacted by treating the general population with hostility.[129] This had the effect of turning the population against them, and led to a cycle of attack and reprisal. Following the evacuation of smaller RIC stations and police huts, the RIC barracks in Toomevara village was the only police station that remained in the vicinity.[130] Commandant Seán Gaynor believed that policemen from that barracks had been making themselves 'very obnoxious in the eyes of the local Volunteers and were going out of their way to provoke trouble'.[131] Volunteer John Hackett recalled in later life that most of the policemen, in particular Sergeant Begley and constables Scanlon and Healy, were 'viciously antagonistic towards the Volunteers'. The acrimony towards these three RIC men arose from incidents during which, it was alleged, they had overstepped their authority by assaulting local militants, in particular Jack Harty, who had received baton injuries in September 1919.[132] A request to the IRA brigade council for permission to shoot the policemen linked to the alleged assault on Harty was refused. However, Brigade Adjutant Seán Gaynor told the Toomevara Volunteers that the refusal should not be taken too seriously. Revealing the tenuous control exercised by GHQ over individual companies, he asserted that most prominent GHQ staff would rather see attacks occurring than having them abandoned for want of official approval, and directed the Volunteers to proceed with an ambush.[133]

During the early weeks of March 1920, a party of Volunteers lay in wait each night on roads out of Toomevara village with the intention of ambushing a police patrol if the opportunity arose. It was then noticed that the police had ceased night patrols as they had become too dangerous. However, they felt able to leave their barracks to attend evening devotions for Lent. A plan was devised to attack them as they left the church. IRA men Paddy Whelehan and John Hackett, both armed with revolvers and wearing disguises, waited outside the church until devotions ended at 7.30 p.m. on the evening of 16 March. Constables Charles Healy and James Rocke were among the congregation, and as they left the church for their barracks they were followed by Whelehan and Hackett, who opened fire on them. Both policemen were badly wounded, and Healy was shot three more times as he lay injured on the roadway. The Volunteers fired extra shots to 'scatter the crowd and prevent themselves from being recognised' before making their escape.[134] They also unintentionally injured fellow IRA Volunteer Con Treacy, who had been attending the same devotions.

Despite his injuries, Healy managed to get back to the barracks, but collapsed in the doorway. He told colleagues that Rocke had been also been shot, but that he forgave the man who shot him. When Begley arrived at the spot where Rocke lay mortally wounded, he found him conscious and continuously saying 'may God forgive them, because I do'.[135] Rocke was brought to the barracks, where two local doctors attended and did everything possible to save the two wounded men.[136] Despite their efforts, Rocke died at 11.15 p.m. and Healy died the following day at a military hospital in Limerick. Within an hour of the shootings, police and military reinforcements arrived from other parts of the county and widespread raids and searches began. Hackett's house and outbuildings were among those searched, and buildings were set ablaze when he could not be located. The village hall in Toomevara was also targeted, with its windows and furniture being smashed.

At the inquest the following morning, Saint Patrick's Day, the coroner remarked that it was a 'sad thing that on the day we all wear the shamrock that we should be here to enquire into the death by violence of fine young Irishmen'.[137] That two policemen had been shot dead as they left a church service caused much controversy and was widely condemned. In his homily during Saint Patrick's Day Mass, Toomevara priest Father Dooley, who had attended the scene and administered the last rites to both men, spoke of seeing an 'innocent young man [Rocke] with his head in the gutter, his blood dyeing the sacred sod from where in happier times the prayers of our holy monks arose to heaven'. He condemned the murderers who had 'branded with their bloody hands the stigma of this crime on the brilliant escutcheon of the parish'. In common with other priests who had condemned the killing of policemen, however, he also placed blame on the government, stating that 'oppression drives the people to desperate methods of defence and revenge'.[138] Three days after the killings, Hackett and eleven other IRA Volunteers, including Whelehan, were arrested and, following periods in jails in Limerick and Belfast, were sent to Wormwood Scrubs prison in London. Along with many other Irish prisoners who were interned without trial, they went on hunger strike, which lasted for twenty-one days before they were released. Following their discharge from prison they returned home to a hero's welcome and rejoined their IRA units.[139]

The government's response to violence, which was to increase the militarisation of the RIC, helped to advance the republican agenda by raising the overall level of violence and discrediting what remained of the public image of the RIC as a civil police force.[140] Reinforcements were urgently needed in Ireland as the conflict escalated, but former Inspector General Byrne had resisted a proposal to recruit former soldiers to the RIC rather than deploy additional troops. He felt that such a force could not be controlled by the constabulary's code of discipline.[141] Inspector General Smyth, however, was a Belfast protestant whose 'unionist sympathies reflected more closely those of colonial office minister, Walter Long'.[142] Recruitment to the new police force began in earnest following Smyth's appointment. The old RIC was already alienated from the community; now it was to be made truly alien by an influx of foreign recruits.[143]

An RIC constable at th
RIC Depot, Phoenix
Park, 1920, in 'marchin
order', equipped with L
Enfield rifle, bayonet an
pouches for cartridges
and handcuffs. *(Courtes
of the Garda Photograph
Section).*

2

An 'Outbreak of Shinnerea': March to December 1920[1]

> 'Anyone passing a police barracks with its locked doors and constables looking out through barred windows will at once realise that no body of men could preserve its morale under such conditions.'[2]

The campaign of intimidation against potential applicants ensured that many Irishmen were reluctant to join the RIC. The consequent decision to recruit non-Irish personnel resulted in the creation of two separate organisations – the Royal Irish Constabulary Special Reserve, colloquially known as 'Black and Tans', and the Auxiliary Division, Royal Irish Constabulary (ADRIC). While the Black and Tans were absorbed into the regular RIC, Auxiliary Division members, termed 'temporary cadets', were former military officers and the division operated in companies of one hundred, each with its own command structure, acting independently of the local police and the military. The mansion of Sir John Carden at Templemore Abbey, which had been vacated when his marriage to Lady Sybil Carden ended in 1902, was occupied by B Company of the Auxiliary Division. It was the only company in Tipperary, and combined with G Company from

Killaloe in County Clare for operations in north Tipperary. South Tipperary was the responsibility of Auxiliary companies based in Kilkenny and north Cork. The introduction of these forces would have a decisive impact on relations between the police and the people of Ireland, especially in counties such as Tipperary, Cork and Dublin, where violence was prevalent.

A temporary shortage of RIC uniforms led to the new arrivals being temporarily issued with a mixture of khaki army and dark green police clothing, which resulted in the epithet 'Black and Tans'. The appearance of these new policemen generated much interest, with the *Tipperary Star* reporting that when the police, attired in 'khaki uniform, but wearing police caps, arrived at Nenagh railway station ... their mixed uniform attracted a considerable amount of attention as they marched to barracks'.[3] The journal of the IRA, *An t-Óglách*, was more outspoken, denouncing the new arrivals as 'physically and morally degenerate Englishmen' and declaring that when the IRA came in contact with them, it would 'make short work of these men'.[4] IRA propaganda portrayed the Black and Tans and Auxiliaries as reprobates, categorising them among other things as the 'sweepings of English gaols', but many were in fact decorated veterans of the First World War. Of the 2,200 men who served in the Auxiliary Division, 633 held gallantry awards, including three with the Victoria Cross, twenty-two with the Distinguished Service Order, 135 with the Military Cross, and twenty-three with the Distinguished Conduct Medal. The new reinforcements had their own outlet for propaganda in the form of the newspaper *The Weekly Summary,* the first issue of which appeared on 5 May 1920. It carried incitements against Sinn Féin members, describing them as murderers and exhorting its readers to make Ireland safe for 'the law-abiding, and an appropriate hell for those whose method is murder'.[5] It also queried whether, if the conflict was considered a war, as the IRA did, 'would it be less war to shoot in his bed the man suspected of having caused the policeman to be shot?' Referring to the arrest of Sinn Féin supporters in Scotland for the possession of arms and ammunition, and the increasing sympathy for the movement internationally, it blamed the worsening situation in Ireland on an 'outbreak of Shinnerea'.[6]

In parallel with the deployment of reinforcements for the police in Ireland, former London Metropolitan Police commissioner General Sir Nevil Macready was appointed commander-in-chief of all Crown forces in Ireland. The press reported that he had been given practically a free hand by the cabinet to suppress the rebellion by whatever means may be requisite.[7] Lord Chancellor Birkenhead stated that special and wholly exceptional steps had been taken to reinforce the police in Ireland.[8] Brigadier General Frank Crozier, commander of the Auxiliary Division, was informed that the new policing organisations were being camouflaged because money could be obtained for police operations, but not for military ones.[9] The Black and Tans and Auxiliary Division soon acquired reputations for brutality and indiscipline. William O'Brien, a former Member of Parliament, described them as 'desperadoes of the vilest type'.[10] Resident Magistrate Sir Christopher Lynch-Robinson, on seeing Black and Tans in person for the first time, compared them to a 'bunch of gorillas with India-rubber looking faces, large ears, big fat lips, and the blank uncanny expression of the cretin'. In contrast, Sir Ormonde Winter, Chief of Intelligence at Dublin Castle, emphasised that most of the new policemen were former soldiers and the conduct of each had been carefully scrutinised before recruitment.[11] To many serving RIC men, the new arrivals were a 'revelation, a plague and a Godsend ... they brought help but they frightened even those that they had come to help'. One Templemore policeman later recalled that the newcomers had neither religion nor morals, they used foul language, had the 'old soldier's talent for dodging and scrounging, spoke in strange accents, called the Irish "natives", associated with low company, stole from one another, sneered at the customs of the country, drank to excess and put sugar on their porridge'.[12] Matters were getting progressively worse for the rank-and-file members of the police, and news that the Treasury had sanctioned the bulk-buying of coffins for the constabulary did not augur well for the future.[13]

On 7 April 1920, a joint operation by the north and mid-Tipperary IRA brigades was mounted to ambush an RIC party that was expected to cycle from Rearcross Barracks to the magistrates' court in the town of Newport. The large IRA ambush party, which included Paddy Ryan (Lacken), Jim Stapleton, Jerry Ryan and Michael Small, believed that the policemen would pass Lackamore Wood on their way to court, so they concealed themselves in the forest and waited. At about 10.30 a.m. three policemen cycled along the isolated and bleak bog road. Constable William Finn and Daniel McCarthy cycled abreast, with Constable Thomas Byrne following closely behind. Byrne later gave evidence that as the policemen passed by the wood, a volley of about twenty shots was fired at them. Byrne was hit, receiving a flesh wound in the upper arm, but he managed to take cover behind a fence. He saw Finn and McCarthy lying on the roadway, and heard McCarthy pleading 'Oh stop, stop,' before more shots rang out. He reported that he recognised local man John Caplis as one of the attackers.

Byrne emptied his revolver into the wood, from where he could see muzzle flashes, and after reloading, he ran from the scene, hearing 'the whizz of bullets' passing very close by him.[14] He again returned fire and managed to escape. As he made his way across the countryside back towards his barracks, he passed two houses where he asked residents for a drink of water, and some cloth to bandage his wound. He was refused assistance, and told in no uncertain terms to leave.[15] Byrne eventually made his way to Lackamore National School, where he took a bicycle, eventually reaching the safety of Newport Barracks. The IRA Volunteers removed weapons and ammunition from the bodies of the dead policemen before leaving the scene.[16]

Later that day a large RIC party under Head Constable Treanor, accompanied by a doctor and priest, went to Lackamore to recover the bodies. The police fired numerous shots into the wood on arrival to ensure that the IRA had left the scene, fearing that they were being lured into another ambush. The bodies of the two dead policemen were recovered and examined, and it was found that both had been badly disfigured by shotgun blasts. Graphic evidence was later given at the inquest that most of Constable Finn's head had been removed by a gunshot, and Constable McCarthy had received multiple gunshot wounds. Treanor reported that he made several arrests, including that of John Caplis, who Constable Byrne alleged had been involved in the attack. His brother, Thomas Caplis, was also arrested, along with the manager of Rearcross creamery, Timothy Kennedy, and Thomas Ryan, who lived beside the scene of the ambush. Treanor described the arrested men as the 'worst kind of Sinn Féiners', singling out Kennedy in particular 'as the principal ringleader of every local villainy'. Considerable hatred existed on both sides and

Treanor admitted in his report to Dublin Castle that the prisoners were taken to the scene and were made to kneel in the blood of the dead policemen, before being forced to kiss the road and pray for their souls. After doing so, they were taken to Limerick and placed in military custody.[17] During the inquest the coroner stated that it would be entirely futile to disguise the fact that they met their deaths in furtherance of the campaign of violence against the police. While he yielded to no man in his condemnation of the government and their military tyranny, he expressed disappointment that County Tipperary should be 'stained with the blood of young Irishmen'. The jury returned verdicts that constables Finn and McCarthy had died from gunshots inflicted by 'some person or persons unknown'.[18]

In March 1920, the IRA carried out a diversionary attack on a temporary RIC hut at Clonoulty, near Thurles. A party of six Volunteers fired at the hut for over two hours under cover of darkness, with one sergeant being wounded in the process. The IRA anticipated that substantial police reinforcements from Thurles would travel towards Clonoulty to relieve the garrison, and made elaborate preparations to ambush them. The main IRA group of twenty-six men dug a trench across the road between Clonoulty and Thurles. Armed with revolvers, shotguns and grenades, they lay in wait to ambush the reinforcements. As the telegraph wires had been cut, policemen inside the hut sent up flares to summon assistance, but none was forthcoming. By this stage of the conflict the RIC was reluctant to respond to such incidents as many policemen had been killed after being lured into ambushes.

With their elaborate plans for an ambush thwarted, the IRA planned another attack, and on 10 May Constable

Patrick McDonnell, who had led the defence of the police hut during the March attack, was shot and killed while on patrol with Constable Hayes near the railway station at Goold's Cross. McDonnell was stationed in Cavan, but he had been temporarily transferred to Tipperary when the situation there deteriorated. His tour of duty in Clonoulty should have ended on 5 May, but his return to Cavan had been delayed because of the injuries received by another policeman. During the inquest, Hayes gave evidence that he and McDonnell had been shot at without warning by four unmasked men armed with rifles and revolvers. He stated that he recognised two of the men as locals John 'Master' Ryan, who was armed with a rifle, and Ned Reilly, who carried a revolver. Hayes managed to flee the scene and continued to return fire as he escaped.[19] He concluded his deposition by saying that he did not know of anyone who had animus towards the sergeant, describing him as 'the quietest man I ever met'.[20] The jury returned a verdict of wilful murder. Descriptions of Ryan and Reilly were circulated in the *Hue and Cry*, the police gazette, and while they were never captured by the RIC, their family homes were burned down in reprisal.

The escalating campaign of boycotting and intimidation affected those who had any connection with the RIC. On 29 April 1920 Bridget O'Toole, a servant at Rearcross Barracks, received a threatening letter warning her that unless she resigned she would suffer the 'extreme penalty'. The letter ended with the sinister remark, 'remember Finn's eyes were missing, so mind yours', a reference to the injuries inflicted on Constable Finn.[21] A young woman in Newport who had ignored IRA warnings to stop keeping company with policemen had her head forcibly shaved as a public humiliation.[22] On 4 June

1920 IRA headquarters issued a boycott order to all Volunteer brigades and companies. An informal boycott against the RIC had been in place for the preceding two years, but General Order Six now officially stipulated that there should be no 'intercourse with the RIC' and that Volunteers must support the boycott of the force as ordered by the Dáil. People who associated with the RIC were to be subject to the same boycott, and any association with the force by them publicised. All IRA members were required to comply with the boycott under threat of being subjected to the same treatment themselves in a 'very obvious and public manner'.[23]

General Order Six placed considerable pressure upon RIC members and their families, as well as on the IRA Volunteers obliged to enforce it. The measure, which followed a decision by the Dáil on 10 April 1920 formally authorising a boycott of the police, particularly affected long-serving members of the RIC. As Irishmen with families and friends living in the country, they were particularly vulnerable to intimidation and boycotting.[24] Each Volunteer company was expected to complete a questionnaire on a monthly basis and submit it to GHQ. The RIC came into possession of a copy when a Volunteer in County Laois was arrested. The document contained instructions relating to the compilation of statistics on the police boycott, with returns to be submitted under the following eight categories:[25]

1. How has the boycott been declared in your area?
2. What are the visible results of the boycott order?
3. Does the general population speak to members of the RIC?

4. Has a list been compiled of persons who are friendly with the police?
5. Are police forced to commandeer supplies?
6. Have merchants been ordered to refuse supplies?
7. What steps have been taken to deal with persons who disobey the boycott order?
8. Have you any suggestions to offer as a means of intensifying the boycott in your area?

The boycott was a powerful expression of the isolation of policemen from their communities and the inspector general wondered how much longer the force could withstand such strain.[26] So too did Limerick-based District Inspector John Regan, who believed that the constabulary was now on the defensive and that the momentum of the IRA was increasing.[27]

As police morale deteriorated, the number of resignations increased from an average of eleven per week in January 1920 to fifty-two per week in June 1920.[28] Reasons given for resignations from the force varied considerably, with some stating they left because of intimidation or fear, while others responded to pressure from family or friends. Some policemen cited ethical or moral reasons for their resignations, such as Constable Daniel Crowley of Clogheen Barracks, near Clonmel. Crowley gave evidence to an American Commission that was investigating allegations of atrocities taking place in Ireland.[29] He claimed that on one occasion, while out on patrol with Black and Tans in an armoured Crossley tender, they received orders that the houses of prominent Sinn Féin members were to be machine-gunned. He further stated that the patrol carried 120 cans of petrol and 120 hand grenades, to be used for the burning of houses and other property during reprisal attacks.

RIC morale suffered another serious setback when a transport embargo commenced in June 1920. Stevedores issued a declaration that they would not handle goods that they regarded as war material arriving at Irish ports. The dockworkers received support in their stance from the Irish Transport and General Workers Union (ITGWU), which led to a railway blockade. The actions of the ITGWU were supported by the English National Union of Railwaymen (NUR). James Henry Thomas, Labour MP and general secretary of the NUR, was the subject of much criticism in the English press for endorsing the embargo against the RIC and military. The police were heavily dependent on rail transport for the supply of materials and reinforcements, and the blockade caused serious disruption. On 21 June, for example, a party of policemen boarded a train at Cloughjordan to travel to Templemore.[30] The driver and guard refused to proceed, citing that they had been directed to do so by their union. The police were ordered to remain on the train so as to break the blockade, but the train remained static at the station for ten days, thus blocking all rail traffic between Roscrea and Limerick.

In July 1920 intelligence was received by the IRA in south Tipperary that a party of policemen regularly travelled from Ballinure Barracks to the nearby town of Cashel to collect pay for distribution. An ambush was planned for the morning of 2 July, when a group of six Volunteers concealed themselves in a meadow surrounded by a wall at Newtown and lay in wait. Shortly afterwards a patrol of six RIC constables on bicycles approached. Shots were fired at the patrol, killing Sergeant Tobin and wounding Constable Brady, but fire was returned by other policemen who found cover. Brady managed to cycle away from the scene, but the four remaining policemen surrendered. They were relieved of their arms, ammunition and bicycles, then allowed to leave.[31] An IRA Volunteer was ordered to follow Brady and shoot him, but when Brady reached a nearby public house he collapsed outside and was surrounded by a large crowd, so he survived. One of those captured at the scene was a Black and Tan named Ross, described in the press as a 'Scotsman dressed in khaki'.[32] Ross later gave evidence at the inquest, and deposed that the IRA had been masked and armed with an assortment of rifles and revolvers, some of which appeared to have been captured RIC weapons. Several of the Volunteers involved in the ambush went on the run immediately afterwards, but Michael Burke, who had been involved, was arrested in August 1920 and later tried by court martial for his involvement.

Following this incident, which subsequently became known as the Newtown ambush, the county inspector for Tipperary reported his belief to Dublin Castle that the renewed and more aggressive IRA campaign in the county arose from the fact that Volunteers in the area had received orders to display more energy from their GHQ.[33] He also noted that the boycotting of the RIC in Tipperary was intensifying. In Templemore, for example, barrack servant Mrs Matthews received a letter ordering her to stop working for the police, and stating that if she failed to do so, she and her family would 'suffer the consequences'. Thurles shopkeepers were also warned against supplying goods to, or having any contact with, the RIC, or they would be subject to the same boycott. Policemen responded to the boycott by commandeering whatever supplies they needed, but the county inspector believed that such tactics, combined with the ongoing attacks, were having a 'deplorable effect on government prestige'.[34]

By the summer of 1920 a pattern had been established whereby isolated rural RIC barracks were evacuated and policemen withdrawn to larger garrisons, which were heavily fortified and easier to defend. The abandoned barracks were usually destroyed by the IRA, serving as potent and visible symbols of the collapse of British administration in Ireland.[35] By July 1920, 343 RIC barracks had been burned, and other government buildings, such as courthouses and revenue offices, were also targeted.[36] As the police withdrew to larger barracks, they recruited men specifically to defend them. Thirty-three former army officers who had served in the Royal Engineers and other specialised regiments were recruited and given the role and title of Defence of Barrack Sergeants. They were not used for regular policing duties, but worked exclusively on defensive measures. Barracks were heavily fortified and surrounded with barbed wire, sandbags, booby traps, and steel shutters and doors. While these measures provided a measure of safety to policemen, it also made their quarters claustrophobic and cramped. To venture outside risked death, but to remain inside brought the threat of siege or other forms of attack. Constabulary reports for the summer of 1920 highlighted significant levels of demoralisation because of the boycott, with some policemen openly calling for the RIC to be disbanded. The inspector general reported that conditions were irksome, depressing and hazardous, a strain that few bodies of men, however highly disciplined, could be expected to bear. He noted the sharp decline in living conditions, the constant danger, and being subjected to the appeals of their parents and families to leave the force: 'they could do little more than defend themselves and their barracks, their lives were a misery'.[37]

A series of large-scale attacks on fortified barracks throughout Ireland occurred during the first half of 1920. The first successful assault involved thirty IRA Volunteers and took place in Ballylanders, County Limerick, on 27 April. The house next door was used to gain access to the roof of the police barracks. Holes were then made in the roof, allowing petrol bombs to be thrown inside. With the police station ablaze, the garrison was forced to surrender. The IRA party were then able to capture all of the police weapons and ammunition. On the same day a similar attack took place in nearby Kilmallock, during which neighbouring IRA brigades combined forces. Two policemen were killed before the garrison finally surrendered. The first attack of this type in Tipperary took place on 26 June in Borrisokane. Elaborate preparations were made in advance, which included cutting the telephone wires and trenching all roads into the town. Over 200 Volunteers took part, over the course of several hours, but they were forced to withdraw when one was killed and another wounded by the police.

Internal feuding in local IRA units was widespread, and some units refused to comply with standing orders from GHQ not to operate within the geographical area of another. As a result, GHQ sent officers to the provinces to professionalise local brigades and battalions. Senior IRA commanders insisted that all plans for attacks on the police or military must first be submitted for approval. This was prompted by the loss of life of some Volunteers who had engaged in what were described as 'half-hearted attempts on posts without proper planning'.[38] Ernie O'Malley was sent by GHQ to Tipperary to plan and lead an attack on Rearcross Barracks. On the night of 12 July

1920, he was in command of over fifty Volunteers, including two of 'the big four' of the Tipperary IRA, Dan Breen and Seán Treacy. As happened in both Ballylanders and Kilmallock, the house adjacent to the barracks was entered and its occupants roused. Commandant Paddy Kinnane later recounted that when the residents were told of the intentions of the IRA, they accepted the position 'cheerfully enough'.[39] Some of the raiding party, including O'Malley and Treacy, went to the roof of the barracks, removed slates and poured paraffin through the hole. When policemen came to investigate, shots were fired at them, forcing them to retreat. Other Volunteers opened fire to prevent the RIC from venturing outside. Despite this fusillade, the barrack door opened and Defence of Barracks Sergeant John Stokes emerged, firing shots at the IRA. This action caused one Volunteer to remark to his colleagues that the policeman was a 'daring devil'. Volunteer Paddy O'Dwyer later recalled that as Stokes returned fire, he collapsed and was dragged back inside by another policeman.[40] Stokes died shortly afterwards. A 21-year-old single man from County Down, he had only one month's service in the RIC, having formerly been an army officer. His bravery was remarked upon by his enemies, who described him as 'courageous to the point of recklessness'.[41] Despite the best efforts of the IRA, the fire that they started did not take hold, and each time the garrison was called on to surrender, the policemen inside responded with volleys of shots.[42] Several members of the raiding party went to the rear yard of the barracks and threw bottles of paraffin on the roof in an attempt to reignite the blaze, but were injured when grenades were thrown from inside. Shrapnel injuries were suffered by several IRA men, including Breen, Treacy and O'Malley, who received the most serious injuries.

Realising that the police were not going to surrender, the IRA withdrew after a siege that had lasted for several hours.

Closing his monthly report for July, the RIC inspector general stated that Tipperary continued to be in a disturbed state, and that the efforts of Sinn Féin were almost wholly directed against the police, in the endeavour to make life unbearable for them and break down the force. He described Munster as by far the worst of all the provinces, with fifteen members of the force murdered during July alone. He referred to threats, boycotting notices and the necessity for policemen to commandeer food. He also stated that the recent establishment of so-called 'Republican Police' and Sinn Féin courts had a serious effect in Tipperary. People who were 'hitherto loyal were obliged to have recourse to the illegal tribunals'. He cautioned that if these courts were allowed to continue with impunity, 'the ordinary law of the realm would be set at nought'.[43]

William Harding Wilson, a native of Ballycumber, King's County (Offaly), joined the RIC in 1882 as a constable, and advanced through the ranks, arriving in Templemore in 1912 as the district inspector. At one stage in his career he had been assigned to the office of the inspector general at RIC headquarters in Dublin Castle. These duties involved him in what were later categorised as 'a good deal of political cases'.[44] Wilson had been in charge of the Templemore police district from 1913 to 1919, when overt displays of defiance and militancy had escalated. Consequently, he had an intimate knowledge of the Volunteer movement and its members in north Tipperary. Both he and District Inspector Hunt in Thurles were deeply resented by the local IRA, and they were targeted for assassination. Following the killing of Hunt in Thurles on 23 June 1920, the assassination of Wilson took priority for local IRA commandant James Leahy, who later described him as 'being on our black books because of his ruthless conduct in the treatment of Republicans'.

The death of Volunteer Captain Michael Small from Borrisoleigh on the night of 3 July 1920 sealed Wilson's fate. An IRA party lay in wait for several hours to attack Shevry Barracks, but a military convoy arrived unexpectedly from Templemore to reinforce the barracks, forcing the attack to be abandoned. Small asked Leahy for permission to return to his home in Upperchurch to attend confession, but as he was travelling across open fields he was observed by a joint RIC and military patrol, which opened fire, wounding him fatally. His body was removed to the morgue at Richmond Barracks in Templemore, and during the inquest medical evidence was given that Small had several gunshot wounds. Commandant Jimmy Leahy attended the inquest and believed from the evidence given that Wilson, who had been in command of the RIC and military patrol, had ordered the firing to begin and was therefore directly responsible for the death of Small. Leahy discussed the issue with other brigade officers and the decision was taken to shoot Wilson 'at any cost and as soon as possible'.

On Monday 16 August 1920 a party consisting of Commandant Paddy Kinnane, Leahy, and Volunteers 'Big' Jim Stapleton, John Fahy and Jack Ryan travelled to Templemore with the intention of killing Wilson. They waited for several hours in various locations near the RIC barracks on the main street. Eventually, they saw Wilson leaving the barracks to walk home. Stapleton, who had also been responsible for the killing of District Inspector Hunt, shot Wilson in the head only yards from the police station, killing him instantly.[45]

That night, 'wild scenes were witnessed' as reprisals took place in Templemore and surrounding areas. The *Tipperary Star* newspaper reported that 'soldiers joined in the outbreak ... volleys were fired along the streets, several houses were attacked, and one shop was looted'.[46] The town hall in Templemore was burned down and creameries at Castleiney, Loughmore and Killea were destroyed.[47] Creameries were a popular target for reprisals by the police and military as their destruction caused disproportionate hardship for a rural population primarily dependent on agriculture. Over one hundred Irish creameries were destroyed between 1919 and 1922.[48]

The burning of Templemore town hall resulted in the deaths of two members of the Northamptonshire Regiment, Captain Sidney Beattie and Lance Corporal H. J. Fuggle. The regimental diary noted that Beattie 'died of accidental injuries' and that Fuggle had 'accidentally burnt to death'.[49] *The Irish Times* reported that Beattie had entered the burning town hall to rescue a trapped civilian with complete disregard for his own safety.[50] *Northampton Daily Chronicle* reported that Beattie had died heroically 'attempting to rescue a man from a fire'.[51] The *Tipperary Star* gave a different version of events, however, and reported that the military had taken petrol at gunpoint from Moynan's garage and when the town hall was set ablaze a cheer was given and a voice shouted 'Sinn Féiners all lie down'.[52] The IRA Volunteers responsible for killing Wilson saw the town hall in Templemore ablaze from their hiding place on the slopes of the Devil's Bit Mountain near the village of Barnane.[53] The following day Volunteer James Duggan visited Templemore and described the 'gruesome spectacle' of the town hall in ashes and the streets strewn with broken glass and debris.[54]

Reporting the death of Wilson to Dublin Castle, County Inspector Dunlop stated his belief that it was his 'fearless manner in dealing with Sinn Féin that led to his death'. He went on to say that the whole efforts of Sinn Féin were directed against the police, and everything conceivable was being done to make the life of policemen 'unbearable'.[55] An inquest was held on 17 August. Nineteen locals were summoned to act as jurors, but only six turned up, and fines were imposed on those who had absented themselves.[56] Wilson was buried at the Church of Ireland cemetery in Templemore on 19 August, with full military honours provided by the Northamptonshire Regiment, which was then garrisoned at Richmond Barracks. Wilson left behind a widow, three sons and a daughter. One of his children was to have been married the following week.[57] His headstone carries the epitaph 'His life for Ireland, his soul for God'.

The death of Beattie in the town hall fire generated much interest, as he was a member of a prominent Dublin family – the son of Sir Andrew Beattie and Lady Beattie of 46 Fitzwilliam Square West.[58] Beattie had been wounded several times during the Great War and awarded the Military Cross while serving with the Northamptonshire Regiment in France in 1917.[59] Sir Andrew was Deputy Lieutenant of Dublin, a former Lord Mayor and also a member of Dublin Corporation. The death of his son led to the passing of a resolution of sympathy by the corporation. Richard Mulcahy, IRA Chief of Staff, was a member of the Sinn Féin group that controlled the corporation, and when news of the resolution reached Tipperary, it 'dumbfounded' local Volunteers. A letter of protest was sent by Jimmy Leahy to Mulcahy, in which he was strongly criticised for not realising that Beattie's death had occurred while he was involved in a reprisal attack, rather than in the heroic rescue of a civilian as had been portrayed in newspaper accounts. He was further criticised for agreeing to support the vote of sympathy. The relationship between Mulcahy and the IRA in Tipperary was already fractious, as the Soloheadbeg ambush had been carried out against the express orders of Mulcahy and IRA headquarters. Leahy heard no more about the matter, although he later recalled his belief that Mulcahy did not like him, even though they had once been on 'friendly terms'.[60] Personal antipathies and clannish feuding within the IRA frequently led to tense relationships between GHQ and local commanders.[61]

Concluding his report to Dublin Castle for August, the RIC inspector general again referred to the bitterness of feeling displayed in Munster and the commitment of the IRA to break the morale of the police. He stated his belief that the IRA viewed the police as 'the last obstacle in the way of the establishment of an Irish Republic'.[62] Notices were posted in several counties denouncing the police as spies and traitors, and warning people not to speak to them or in any way tolerate their existence, under penalty of death. As the cycle of reprisal and counter-reprisal continued, the military occasionally found innovative ways to turn the tables on their enemy. For example, the IRA regularly engaged in the practice of blocking roads by digging trenches and felling trees prior to staging an ambush. In Templemore, the Northamptonshire Regiment discouraged this practice by forcing the nearest inhabitants to saw up the wood and deliver it to the barracks. One officer noted that while 'the innocent may have suffered for the guilty, it was noticeable that tree-felling rapidly became less popular'.[63]

After the death of Wilson and consequent reprisals, the local population was fearful of what might happen next. The town was thrown into further turmoil when sixteen-year-old farm labourer James Walsh claimed that he was experiencing Marian apparitions. It was alleged that religious statues owned or touched by him were shedding tears of blood in the shop of newsagent Thomas Dwan, in the nearby RIC barracks and in a cottage owned by Dwan's sister-in-law Miss Maher in the townland of Curraheen, near where Walsh lived. Thousands of pilgrims visited the town each day and for several weeks Templemore became a place of pilgrimage on a par with Knock or Lourdes. James Walsh also alleged that a 'holy well' had appeared in the floor of his bedroom. The *Tipperary Star* reported that, after the reprisals of Monday 16 August, some of the statues from which blood had been oozing had been taken by Walsh to Templemore, and many locals believed that this action had saved the town from destruction.[64] The *Limerick Leader* reported that prominent townsmen assembled around the statues and prayed aloud, thanking God that the town was saved and that none of the 'inoffensive townspeople suffered any further'. Devout locals claimed that 'our Lady had saved Templemore'.[65]

On 31 August 1920, County Inspector Dunlop from Nenagh reported the bizarre situation in Templemore to Dublin Castle. He stated that on 20 August miraculous apparitions were supposed to have appeared in Templemore and Curraheen. Religious statues belonging to Jimmy Walsh and RIC Constable Thomas Wimsey from Templemore were alleged to be bleeding, and several miraculous cures had taken place.[66] The *Tipperary Star* reported that the statue had been given to Wimsey by Jimmy Walsh several weeks earlier, and had been kept in his quarters in the RIC barracks. When news spread that a bleeding statue was inside the barracks, it was besieged by a large crowd of pilgrims. Some entered the building and had to be forcibly removed by the police.[67] Following this incident, Dunlop had the statue removed from the barracks and placed with the other statues on an improvised altar that had been erected in the yard beside Dwan's shop on Main Street. Wimsey left the RIC shortly afterwards and told the *Tipperary Star* that he intended to join a religious order.[68] The relevant extract from the RIC service register shows that Wimsey, a Roman Catholic from Mayo who had joined the RIC in 1913, resigned from the force on 7 September 1920.[69] Jimmy Walsh was not known to the local RIC or to have had any involvement with the Irish Volunteers or Sinn Féin before these incidents began, but his brother had been arrested for militant activity and imprisoned without charge or trial in Wormwood Scrubs prison in London, where he had gone on hunger strike.[70]

Dunlop reported that a pilgrimage to Templemore had started from all parts of Ireland, with many thousands thronging daily into the town.[71] He further reported that the alleged miracles were having a positive effect on the locality, describing the conduct of the large crowds as 'exemplary'. Newspapers renamed Templemore as 'Pilgrimville' or 'Pilgrimstown'. To cater for the pilgrims, who were described by one newspaper as 'the halt, the maim and the blind', additional trains were scheduled to run to Templemore from Kingsbridge Station in Dublin.[72] By 4 September, the RIC estimated that in excess of 15,000 people per day were making the pilgrimage to Templemore, and then on to the cottage at Curraheen. The cottage was regarded as being as much a place of pilgrimage as Templemore because of the reported existence of the holy well in the floor of Walsh's bedroom.[73] The throng of pilgrims prompted one elderly local to make an analogy with the Klondike Gold Rush of 1897–98, which he had experienced, remarking that in August 1920 ''twas easier to get from Skagway to the Klondike' than from Templemore to Curraheen.[74] The influx of visitors brought a significant economic windfall to the area, which one newspaper stated 'must have done better than many a seaside town in Ireland this year'.[75]

Many members of the clergy visited Templemore, including Archbishop Patrick Clune of Perth diocese, Western Australia. Clune was acting as an intermediary in secret negotiations that were taking place between the British government and representatives of Sinn Féin. During his time in Templemore, Clune met senior IRA commanders, including Jimmy Leahy, but when the time came to depart he was unable to do so because of the huge numbers of pilgrims. Clune approached the IRA for assistance and Leahy commandeered a car that had brought pilgrims from Galway to Templemore, instructing the driver to take the Archbishop to Limerick. On arrival, Clune offered payment to the driver, who refused to accept it. When Clune asked why he would not take the payment, he replied 'sure wasn't I commandeered in the name of the Republic!'[76]

Reporting to IRA GHQ on the surreal events in Templemore, Vice Commandant Edward McGrath, of the Second Tipperary Brigade, said that the town was packed with 'pilgrims, beggars, stall-holders and undesirables'. He noted that the police and military had disappeared off the streets and that the IRA appeared to be in charge. They controlled traffic and parking, and restored order.[77] It was as if an informal truce or understanding had been reached between the IRA, the military and the police due to the extraordinary circumstances which prevailed. IRA Volunteers acted as stewards to control the large number of pilgrims, but did not appear on the streets in uniform. However, the IRA did use the absence of the military and the police to survey potential targets and suitable locations for future ambushes.

Jimmy Leahy imposed a levy of two shillings and six pence per day on all cars bringing pilgrims from Templemore to the cottage at Curraheen. The 'pilgrim tax' was imposed to pay for repairs to roads, which had been badly damaged by the large crowds, and also to pay the expenses of IRA Volunteers involved in traffic and crowd control. The imposition of the levy caused an outcry, and Count O'Byrne, Sinn Féin TD and chairman of north Tipperary County Council, demanded to meet Leahy and other IRA commanders. O'Byrne stated that the levy was highly irregular. Leahy replied that 'everything had to be irregular to deal with the situation that had arisen'.[78] O'Byrne suggested that the council should take over the collection of the levy, but Leahy refused, saying that he intended to buy arms and ammunition with any balance left over after deducting the legitimate expenses of the Volunteers.[79] The *Limerick Leader* reported that pilgrims were loud in their praise of the 'splendid men of Óglaigh na nÉireann' who maintained order and prevented excessive profiteering by shopkeepers, caterers and hoteliers.[80] Collection boxes on behalf of the IRA and Cumann na mBan were placed along the pilgrimage route between Templemore and Curraheen, and gathered over £1,500 in contributions from pilgrims.

Several days after the miracles began, Leahy and other brigade officers arranged a private interrogation of Jimmy Walsh. They had started to view the bizarre incidents with scepticism and were also seriously concerned that Volunteer discipline was being compromised. Leahy later recalled that pilgrims had begun to give lavish tips to IRA Volunteers, and that some who had previously been abstemious and enthusiastic took to drink and began to forget that they were engaged in a 'life and death struggle' for freedom. A meeting took place in Dwan's house between Walsh and an IRA delegation led by Leahy. Walsh told Leahy that when he had last spoken to the apparition, the Virgin Mary had indicated her approval of IRA guerrilla tactics, including the shooting of policemen, and wished to see the campaign intensified. Leahy later recalled that he found it difficult 'to keep a straight face' and concluded that Walsh was either 'mentally abnormal or a hypocrite'.[81] Following this meeting, the IRA leadership decided that conclusive action should be taken to halt the influx of pilgrims and bring the phenomenon of the Templemore miracles to an end.

Leahy contacted Michael Collins directly and expressed his concern about the situation in Templemore and the detrimental effect it was having on Volunteer discipline and military operations in the area. Collins ordered Dan Breen to interrogate Walsh, to which Breen reluctantly agreed.[82] Neither Collins nor Breen were renowned for their piety or religious devotion, and Collins in particular had a reputation for being actively anti-clerical. His maiden political speech in London in 1908 was described as a 'violent attack upon the influence of the Catholic hierarchy and clergy'.[83] Walsh was brought from Templemore to O'Neill's pub in Dublin, a safe haven for Tipperary IRA men. While waiting to see Breen, some of the more devout IRA members present insisted on kissing Walsh's coat and addressing him as 'saint'. Commandant Dinny Lacey of the Third Tipperary Brigade requested of Walsh that the next time he 'spoke to the Blessed Virgin Mary, be sure to insist on nothing less than a republic'. Breen interrogated Walsh for fifteen minutes and concluded that he was faking the miracles. Collins was briefed by Breen about his questioning of Walsh and his opinion that the apparitions and miracles were not genuine. Collins sarcastically replied 'one can't take any notice of what you say Breen, because you have no religion'.[84]

Leahy visited Canon Ryan in Thurles and requested that the alleged apparitions and cures be denounced from the pulpit, to deter pilgrims from travelling to Curraheen, but this request was refused.[85] Tensions already existed between the church and the IRA over Cardinal Logue, Primate of All Ireland, remarking of the Volunteers in 1918 that 'no object would excuse them, no hearts, unless hardened and steeled against pity, would tolerate their cruelty'.[86] Having been rebuffed by the church, the IRA took violent and decisive action to end the influx of pilgrims. An ambush was carried out on 29 September 1920 near the RIC barracks at Golding's Cross on the pilgrimage route, in the course of which constables Edward Noonan and Terence Flood were shot dead. Constables Marnane and Ferris were wounded, but managed to escape. Flood was initially reported missing, but later found at Gortalough near Templemore, 'his body riddled with bullets'.[87] After the ambush, a party of pilgrims was stopped by the IRA and ordered to place the body of Constable Noonan in their car and deliver it to Richmond Barracks in Templemore.[88] It was reported that many local residents left the area following the ambush, fearing a repetition of the reprisals that had taken place after the death of District Inspector Wilson several weeks earlier.[89]

Collins remained curious. He instructed Seán Harling, a commandant in the second battalion of the Dublin Brigade of

Fianna Éireann, who worked as a courier for Dáil Éireann, to travel to Tipperary and return with one of the bleeding statues. Collins had received complaints from a local priest that IRA Volunteers had engineered the statues so that they would bleed at specific times. Harling recalled that when he returned to Dublin, Collins examined the statue at length, then took hold of it and hit it off the side of the desk, at which the works of an alarm clock fell out. A mechanism had been concealed inside the statue, which was connected to fountain pen inserts containing a mixture of sheep's blood and water. When the clock mechanism struck a certain time it would send a spurt of blood through the statue's heart, giving the impression that the statue was bleeding. 'I knew it,' said Collins.[90]

As the IRA had intended, news of the ambush brought a substantial number of military and police reinforcements into the area. *The Freeman's Journal* reported that they engaged in a 'reign of terror' by indiscriminately firing into houses and across fields.[91] Soldiers from the Northamptonshire Regiment went to the 'holy well' in Curraheen and also to Dwan's yard in Templemore, where they removed crutches and other items left behind by pilgrims. Some soldiers decorated themselves with religious artefacts, while others feigned lameness and began using the crutches, parading around the streets in mockery of the supposed cures. Rumours spread that Templemore would be burned to the ground as a reprisal for the deaths of constables Noonan and Flood, causing the remaining 'pilgrims, stall-holders and tramps' to leave the area quickly.[92] Thus, the phenomenon of the 'Templemore miracles' ended as suddenly as it had begun.

Following his interrogation by Breen, Walsh was taken to the Salesian College at Pallaskenry, Limerick, and placed in the care of Father Aloysius Sutherland, at the request of clergy from Templemore. In 1923 Walsh emigrated to Australia, initially staying with relatives in Melbourne, and eventually settling in Sydney. The 1932 census for Sydney gives his occupation as 'medical student'.[93] By the 1950s his marriage had ended, his teenage son had died tragically young, and Walsh was employed as a lay teacher in a Roman Catholic school. In a remarkable coincidence, he was recognised by a visiting Irish Christian Brother who had been in Templemore at the time of the miracles over thirty years earlier.[94] The matter was reported to the cardinal, who expressed his concern that 'Walsh might be a dangerous type of person to have teaching in one of our Catholic schools'.[95] The diocese contacted the New South Wales police seeking information that could be used to dismiss Walsh from his teaching post. The police had no negative information on Walsh, but nonetheless he was dismissed by the Catholic Church. After his sacking, Jimmy Walsh was employed as a hospital porter, but he spent the rest of his life trying to enter various religious orders, even becoming a novice in a Benedictine monastery. He was unsuccessful in these attempts, however, because he was divorced. Jimmy Walsh died after a prolonged illness on 12 March 1977, and was buried in Sydney. He never returned to Ireland.[96]

The brief interlude that saw Templemore become a world-famous place of pilgrimage lasted only a few weeks, and the Kiloskehan ambush brought about a swift and violent resumption of hostilities. On 28 October a military convoy travelling from Templemore was ambushed at Thomastown, near Tipperary town. The engagement between the military and the IRA lasted for almost an hour and resulted in the deaths of three soldiers. Newspapers reported that much bitterness prevailed among the rank and file of the regiment at the loss of their comrades, and this manifested itself in reprisal attacks carried out in Templemore and Tipperary town.[97] For the second time in a few weeks, Templemore was badly damaged. Masked men wearing trench coats appeared on the streets, shouting anti-Sinn Féin slogans such as 'We will have revenge' and 'Up the Black and Tans'.[98] Several shops were looted before being set ablaze. County Inspector Dunlop reported that the Thomastown ambush had led to 'reprisals by armed and disguised men, resulting in serious loss of property', but made no reference to the identity of those who led them. The police, including the Black and Tans, did not join in the reprisals, but intervened to bring them to an end by forcing the soldiers back to the barracks at gunpoint, and also assisted by putting out fires. During the attack terrified townspeople were allowed to take refuge in the RIC barracks, and the police were subsequently thanked by the local urban district council for their actions.[99]

Reprisals carried out by Crown forces provoked local, national and international criticism, and led to the perception, as articulated in *The Times*, that 'either the executive authority regards them with a certain leniency or that it is powerless to stop them'. Commenting on the effect of reprisals on the civilian population, the RIC county inspector blamed the IRA, stating that when they committed an outrage 'no steps [were] taken to protect the locality from the consequences'.[100] The government suppressed Sinn Féin and what were described as 'kindred associations' under the Criminal Law and Procedure (Ireland) Act. In the martial-law areas of Clare and Tipperary, public assemblies, including fairs and markets, were prohibited under the Defence of the Realm regulations.[101]

Several key events took place on the national stage during this period that had consequences for the conflict in Tipperary. On 14 October 1920, Seán Treacy, one of 'the big four' of the Tipperary IRA, was shot dead in an exchange of fire with members of the Auxiliary Division on Talbot Street in Dublin. Three other people, including a child, were also killed in the crossfire. In London, Terence MacSwiney, Lord Mayor of Cork, died on 25 October after spending seventy-three days on hunger strike. In Dublin, eighteen-year-old medical student Kevin Barry was executed on 1 November for his involvement in an attack on a military patrol that resulted in the death of a soldier. His youthfulness and background made his death a cause célèbre, generating widespread sympathy and adding to the pressure on the government to reach a negotiated settlement. These events triggered a renewed IRA offensive in both Munster and Dublin.[102]

In Tipperary, orders were received from IRA GHQ that, in reprisal for the actions of the British government in allowing MacSwiney to die, at least one policeman should be shot in each battalion area.[103] In the town of Cloughjordan, IRA Volunteers had great antipathy towards local policemen. Commandant Seán Gaynor later recounted his belief that they had been 'overly aggressive' towards Volunteers as the conflict escalated. Information was received that some policemen were in the habit of drinking at night in Tooher's Hotel in the town, and plans were made to ambush them. It was intended that a local Volunteer would identify certain policemen, believed to be 'objectionable characters', who would then be shot. On the night of 2 November four IRA men entered the hotel but were noticed by two policemen who were drinking inside the premises. Constable Savage managed to escape, but

Constable Maxwell was shot dead while attempting to draw his revolver. The houses of the Volunteers involved in the killing were searched later that night, but all had gone on the run and escaped capture. Aged twenty-four, Maxwell had been a policeman for only five months, having been a soldier for several years. A single man, his body was returned to his native County Down for burial.

On the same evening, Constable McCarthy was shot and badly wounded in Nenagh. Two houses belonging to prominent IRA members in the town were destroyed in reprisal. Other houses were searched, including the presbytery of local curate Father O'Halloran – an 'outspoken critic of British rule, even from the pulpit'.[104] During the search of the presbytery it was alleged that Lieutenant H. J. Hambleton, intelligence officer of the First Battalion, Northamptonshire Regiment, had threatened to shoot O'Halloran. This allegation was sufficient to ensure that Hambleton was selected for assassination. He was known to use a motorcycle to travel from Summerhill Barracks in Nenagh, where he was based, to the regimental headquarters at Richmond Barracks in Templemore. When an IRA Volunteer working in the fields saw Hambleton travelling towards Templemore on his motorcycle, an ambush was swiftly arranged and an IRA party waited at Lisstunny near Nenagh for his return journey. Hambleton was wounded by the first volley of shots and attempted to return fire, but he was shot again as he lay on the ground. Patrick Cash, a member of the ambush party, later said that his dying words were 'You bastards, you got me at last.'[105] When Volunteers searched his body for documents and ammunition, he was found to be wearing steel body armour, similar to the type that had been worn by British troops in the trenches during the Great

War. The official history of the Northamptonshire Regiment stated that, in his role as an intelligence officer, Lieutenant Hambleton had 'shown himself to be absolutely fearless and had become a marked man'.[106] Hambleton had worked closely with a local RIC district inspector, who local Volunteers believed appeared to suffer from 'cold feet' after his death.[107]

When his remains arrived in Nenagh, some of his soldiers became incensed by the sight of his dead body, and set fire to several premises, including the local creamery.[108] Shots were fired, grenades thrown, and broken glass littered the streets. The cost of the damage was estimated at £2,000. Protestant and Catholic clergy in the town united with local businessmen and sent a telegram to Dublin Castle asking for 'protection for panic-stricken townspeople'.[109] In a follow-up search by the military for suspects at Knigh Cross, between Puckane and Nenagh, four local men were arrested. Volunteers John O'Brien and Thomas O'Brien of the Nenagh Company were killed shortly afterwards.[110] The IRA alleged that both men had been bayoneted to death while under arrest, and their bodies dumped at the roadside. The military issued a standard response of the time, which was to claim that both men had been shot 'while trying to escape'.[111]

In Dublin, 'the squad' assembled by Michael Collins delivered a significant blow to the intelligence network in Ireland when twelve British military officers were shot dead and several others wounded on the morning of 21 November in an audacious operation. British Army headquarters conceded that 'temporary paralysis of the secret service had occurred after the killings'.[112] Revenge followed swiftly, when the Auxiliary Division killed twelve people and seriously wounded a further eleven during a football match at Croke

Park. This event became known as Bloody Sunday and proved to be a substantial propaganda coup for the militant republican movement.

Of the 178 RIC policemen killed in Ireland during 1920, twenty were killed in County Tipperary. Besides the dramatic statistics of actual deaths, new categories in police reports introduced in April 1920 revealed the extent of intimidation and boycotting against the RIC and people associated with them. Writing about the effect of the boycott on individual policemen, one RIC commander noted that 'it hits them hard ... as it is intended to prevent the necessities of life'.[113] National statistics for the period from April to December illustrate the scale of the campaign:

Outrage and intimidation statistics, April–December 1920

Policemen wounded	465
Policeman fired at or attacked (without injury)	408
Policemen threatened	215
RIC candidates intimidated or threatened	57
Policemen's families attacked or threatened	153
Police suppliers or landlords intimidated or threatened	802

Such incidents placed the counter-insurgency campaign on a new footing. Internment was reintroduced, curfews were extended and huge numbers of checkpoints, searches and arrests took place. The inspector general reported to the chief secretary that during November there had been no abatement of the Sinn Féin conspiracy to 'set the law at defiance' and render British rule ineffective in Ireland in pursuance of the claim to national independence.[114] For rank-and-file members of the constabulary, morale was difficult to sustain. Aside from the constant fear of death or injury, hundreds of experienced policemen had resigned or retired. The recruitment of Black and Tans and the Auxiliary Division, measures that had been intended to improve the situation, had made matters substantially worse. The campaign of intimidation aimed at the families, friends and associates of the police made them legitimate targets for the IRA, and that constant threat added to the severe pressures on serving members, who did not have the luxury of only having to worry about their own safety. Patrick Shea, the son of an RIC sergeant in Tipperary, later recognised that he had no knowledge of the dilemma of a father who had a family to care for: 'the possibility that he might give up his job was never in my mind. I was at the age when the props of life are permanent and unchanging; my father was a member of the RIC and for better or worse that was that'.[115]

An RIC constable at the RIC Depot, Phoenix Park, 1920. He is likely a Black anc Tan as he carries a revolver in military 'cross draw' style, and his medal ribbons indicate extensive military service. *(Courtesy of the Garda Photographic Section).*

3

The Storm before the Calm: January to July 1921

> 'Picture constables out of bed every night ... and not knowing the moment that a bullet or bomb may come through one of the windows and send them to eternity'[1]

The autumn and winter of 1920 brought about a significant change in the tactics of the IRA in Tipperary and other counties with high levels of violence. IRA Chief of Staff Richard Mulcahy wrote in later life of his frustration at the lack of military discipline in the three Tipperary brigades.[2] To counter such indiscipline, he despatched staff officers, including Ernie O'Malley, from IRA headquarters to rural areas with the intention of professionalising the military wing of the Volunteers. Increased levels of police and military activity had forced many IRA men to leave their homes and employment, going 'on the run'. These men then became the nuclei of full-time forces described as 'active service units' by IRA headquarters, and perhaps better known colloquially as 'flying columns'. Initially, these columns formed spontaneously in the most violent counties because of the conditions that prevailed at the time, but approval was given by GHQ to extend the concept into each brigade area. The structure of these columns allowed greater flexibility in the planning and execution of ambushes. Consequently, the number of successful ambushes carried out by the IRA increased substantially, culminating in an incident on 28 November 1920 at Kilmichael, County Cork, when eighteen members of the Auxiliary Division were killed by a flying column led by Tom Barry. IRA Volunteers now received professional training in supervised camps, allowing the officer corps to be improved, with competent officers promoted and incompetent ones removed.[3]

The introduction of flying columns led to a change in tactics from symbolic attacks on heavily fortified RIC barracks to strategically chosen ambushes on mobile patrols and convoys. While attacks on barracks had exposed inexperienced Volunteers to the use of arms, others felt that even if it was 'a relief from boredom, it provided little more than firing practice'.[4] The first major operation of the Third Tipperary Brigade flying column was the Thomastown ambush of 28 October 1920, when three soldiers of the Northamptonshire Regiment were shot dead. The county inspector for Tipperary south alluded to the new development in his November report, when he referred to 'bands of men at work ... with the exclusive object of ambushing police or military'. He went on to confirm that these bands consisted of men who, for various reasons, were on the run. He suggested that flying columns were not popular with the majority of the country people, but they were 'ruled by terror'.[5] Another large-scale attack was planned for November on a police convoy that regularly travelled between the villages of Bansha and Galbally. On 13 November 1920, after several abortive attempts, a flying column of sixteen Volunteers under Commandant Dinny Lacey lay in wait at Inches Cross in the Glen of Aherlow. Just after 3 p.m. a lorry containing eight policemen drove into the ambush. Lacey blew a whistle, which was the signal to commence firing. The driver was killed in the first fusillade, which caused the lorry to crash into a ditch. An exchange of fire ensued, during which three more policemen were killed. One managed to escape and sought refuge at a nearby cottage where he requested assistance, but none was forthcoming.[6] The engagement lasted for about ten minutes before the remaining constables surrendered. Their weapons and ammunition were taken and the lorry set ablaze before the flying column left the scene. Constables Charles Bustrock, Patrick Mackessy, John Miller and Jeremiah O'Leary were killed, and all of the policemen who survived the ambush were wounded.

Reprisals swiftly followed. Several premises were set ablaze, including the cottage of John Burke, where shelter had been refused to the policeman who had fled the scene.[7] Newspapers subsequently reported that reprisals had been carried out by armed men dressed in civilian clothing.[8] Such incidents were officially classed by the RIC as 'rioting', with no blame apportioned, but local IRA Volunteers were in no doubt that the attacks were carried out by policemen and soldiers.[9] Dealing with the sensitive and controversial issue of reprisals, Field Marshal Sir Henry Wilson, Chief of the Imperial General Staff, wrote to Prime Minister Lloyd George, setting out his view that a coordinated series of official reprisals should take place. He concluded that reprisals were being carried out without permission, stating that if IRA men were to be murdered, 'then the government ought to murder them'.[10]

For Volunteers, the topography of Tipperary was an important feature in determining suitable locations for ambushes. The historian of the British Army's 6th Division wrote that it was noticeable how areas in and around mountains were the most disaffected.[11] Variously described as 'wild mountain country' or a 'bleak and desolate place', the village of Kilcommon and the surrounding area provided the ideal setting for the guerrilla warfare that had been adopted, and was now being perfected, by the IRA.[12] In this rugged area, the attack on Rearcross Barracks, the Lackamore Wood ambush, and numerous other less lethal encounters had taken place. IRA flying columns had the crucial advantage of comprehensive local knowledge, making this part of north Tipperary home to some of the most dangerous police districts in Ireland. An important tactic utilised by the IRA throughout Ireland was the interception of mail intended for the police or military, and mailbags were regularly taken at gunpoint from trains or deliverymen. Following such seizures, mail intended for barracks as well as personal mail for policemen was removed before mail intended for residents and local businesses was returned. To counteract this development, the police began to collect mail from post offices, but doing so presented an opportunity for the IRA to attack them. While the routes taken were changed regularly, the police were at their most vulnerable as they left barracks, or coming to and from post offices.

On 16 December 1920 the IRA First Brigade flying column assembled with the intention of attacking the police as they left Kilcommon Barracks to make the 1-mile journey to the post office at Kilcommon Cross. As the ambushers lay in wait, snow began to fall, but they had brought several bottles of *poitín*, and one Volunteer later recalled that a 'good swig helped to keep the cold out'.[13] At about 10 a.m. scouts reported that a patrol of eight men on foot had left the barracks and was heading towards Kilcommon Cross. Under the command of a sergeant who was well known to the IRA and who they were keen to shoot, the policemen approached the ambush site in pairs, ten paces apart.[14] A shot was fired prematurely by one Volunteer, removing the element of surprise. The RIC dispersed, with some seeking cover to return fire while others tried to run back towards their barracks. Two policemen were killed instantly and two more died as they tried to reach safety. Police inside the station opened fire at the ambushers and also sent up flares to summon assistance from Newport Barracks, 12 miles away. The IRA attempted to take rifles and ammunition from the dead policemen, but they were forced to abandon the attempt as fire was being returned from the police barracks. The IRA Volunteers, most of whom had also been involved in the attack on Rearcross Barracks and the Lackamore ambush, moved cross-country, anticipating the reprisals that would inevitably follow. The four policemen who died in the ambush were constables Patrick Halford, Ernest Harden, Albert Palmer and Arthur Smith. All had fewer than nine months' RIC service. The sergeant who was the primary target of the attack managed to escape, much to the disappointment of the Volunteers, and two wounded policemen were brought to Nenagh hospital for treatment.[15] Reprisals swiftly followed, and it was reported that 'panic-stricken people fled from their homes on hearing of the ambush'.[16] Several buildings in the area, including the home of William Hanly, who had taken part in the ambush, were set ablaze in the immediate aftermath.

The RIC believed that the significant increase in the level of IRA activity in south Tipperary during late 1920 was due to Dan Breen having assumed command in the area. The county inspector stated that 'as long as this man is at large constant attacks on police and military are to be expected'.[17] Having been in Dublin for several months recuperating from gunshot wounds, Breen had returned to Tipperary just before Christmas 1920 and rejoined the Third Brigade, but in a very limited capacity due to his injuries. In his absence the IRA had maintained constant pressure on the police, and the RIC barracks at Glenbower, 5 miles from Carrick-on-Suir, became a particularly dangerous posting. Volunteers 'made it a practice to snipe twice a week at the garrison ... to keep their nerves on edge'.[18] This had the desired effect, but led to a tragic incident on 19 December 1920, when two police patrols opened fire on each other in the darkness, resulting in the death of one policeman and the severe wounding of another. A patrol of military cyclists travelling from Mullinahone to Carrick-on-Suir was fired on at Ninemilehouse, wounding four soldiers. As the soldiers returned to Mullinahone to raise the alarm, a military patrol from Callan and a police patrol from Kilkenny set out for the scene of the ambush. Both patrols arrived at the townland of Kilbride simultaneously, and the Callan contingent, not recognising the other party as police in the darkness, called on the Kilkenny patrol to halt.[19] The Kilkenny patrol, believing that they had run into an ambush, opened fire. Sergeant Thomas Walsh was shot dead and Sergeant Thomas Shannon was badly wounded in the exchange of fire, which continued for some time before both sides realised what had occurred.

Initial reports of the incident carried exaggerated claims that there had been three separate ambushes and that many soldiers and IRA Volunteers had been killed or wounded. Owing to official reticence, it was difficult to ascertain the facts of what had taken place, but it was reported that 'the greatest alarm prevailed in the district', as residents prepared themselves for possible reprisal.[20] Some were reported to be in 'a state of intense terror ... with many fleeing their homes'. Sergeant Walsh, a single 42-year-old man from Ballyragget, had twenty years' police service and had just been promoted to the rank of sergeant. As his cortège passed through Callan, residents were ordered to remain indoors and businesses to close their doors as a mark of respect. One publican who failed to do as directed was shot at and wounded.[21]

The most active IRA Volunteers had now become full-time members of flying columns, greatly increasing their professionalism and military efficiency. Counties Cork, Tipperary, Kerry and Limerick, together with the cities of Cork and Limerick, were placed under martial law. General Sir Nevil Macready declared that a state of armed insurrection existed in Ireland, and that while Great Britain had no quarrel with Irishmen, 'her sole quarrel is with crime, outrage, and disorder; her sole object in declaring martial law is to restore peace to a distracted and unhappy country; her sole enemies are those who have countenanced, inspired and participated in rebellion, murder, and outrage'.[22] In a separate development, many Volunteers who were also devout Roman Catholics were shocked when Bishop Colohan of Cork announced that the killers of policemen would be excommunicated. In a pastoral letter, he stated that the killing of police was morally murder and politically of no consequence, and that the burning of barracks was simply the 'destruction of Irish property'.[23]

The road from Templemore to Nenagh via the village of Borrisoleigh was one of the most dangerous roads in Tipperary between 1919 and 1922. Stretching 21 miles in length, the road meandered through valleys and wooded countryside, making it ideal for ambushes. The Northamptonshire Regiment had a large garrison at Summerhill Barracks in Nenagh, and the county inspector of the RIC was also based in the town. This meant that frequent journeys between Templemore and Nenagh were necessary for both the military and the police. Many ambushes took place at various points on the road, leading soldiers to name it 'happy valley' or 'the valley of death'.[24] To deter the IRA from attacking their lorries, the military adopted the tactic of carrying 'one or more prominent Sinn Féiners on all motor convoys'. This practice was also adopted in other counties known for frequent attacks on the police and military, though the county inspector for Tipperary north expressed doubts that it would bear good results, feeling that it merely encouraged Volunteers to go on the run.[25]

In December 1920, IRA Commandant Edward McGrath was interned in Richmond Barracks in Templemore under the provisions of the Restoration of Order in Ireland Act. He was visited in his cell by Captain Phipps of the Northamptonshire Regiment, who informed him that he would be brought as a hostage on military transports.[26] McGrath was taken out on several occasions and forced to walk in front of the trucks as they travelled through 'the valley of death', between Borrisoleigh and Nenagh. On one occasion the convoy was attacked and McGrath suffered the ignominy of seeking cover in a ditch to avoid being shot by his comrades. From his vantage point, McGrath had a close view of the soldiers' reactions to this form of guerrilla warfare and later observed that the 'British Tommies were simply terrified'.[27] At Christmas 1920, a large party of IRA Volunteers led by Jim Stapleton, the man who had shot district inspectors Hunt and Wilson, ambushed a military convoy at Collaun, between Nenagh and Borrisoleigh. The convoy consisted of fifteen trucks and over 150 soldiers. This engagement lasted from 9 a.m. until 3 p.m., when the Volunteers withdrew, fearing the arrival of reinforcements from Templemore. Following this ambush, the route was no longer used by the military or the police.

As 1920 drew to a close, an upsurge in violence took place, with the situation in the county being described as 'most unsatisfactory' by the county inspector. On 6 December 1920 the Provincial Bank in Templemore was raided and over £3,000 stolen. The county inspector attributed this incident to a Sinn Féin fundraising exercise, but he also made the point that a number of crimes were being committed by 'young hooligans who have seized the opportunity which the existing state of the county gives'.[28] When 1921 began, policemen serving in Tipperary who hoped their situation might improve were to be disappointed. They continued to live a wretched existence in fortified barracks, risking death each time they ventured outside, while the parallel campaign of intimidation and boycotting against them and their families continued. Tipperary in 1921 was a very dangerous county for serving or retired members of the RIC, applicants to the force, and anyone with a connection to the police. The inspector general complained that people with information about the IRA 'were afraid to say anything for fear that they will be suspected and murdered by the rebels'.[29]

In January 1921, as a response to IRA guerrilla tactics, military transports were covered for the first time with steel plates and protected with wire netting to repel hand grenades.[30] In reaction to the imposition of martial law, the IRA reorganised and formed new divisions, with Ernie O'Malley becoming divisional commandant for north Tipperary. The first Tipperary RIC death of 1921 took place on 17 January at Cappawhite. Constable Robert Boyd was drinking in Mrs Moran's bar when four IRA Volunteers entered and shot him four times, killing him instantly. Mrs Moran's niece suffered a leg wound from a ricocheting bullet. A former soldier from Banbridge, County Down, Boyd had been in the RIC for only ten months. His father and two brothers also served in the force. Following his death, two shops in Cappawhite were burned down and all fairs, markets and public assemblies were forbidden while the pattern of ambushes and reprisals continued unabated.

On 10 February 1921, RIC Constable John Carroll went to visit his parents at their farm in Ballywilliam near Nenagh. Carroll was stationed in Cork, but he had found himself unexpectedly in Nenagh as part of a police convoy travelling to Cork city from the RIC Depot in Dublin's Phoenix Park. When the convoy stopped for the night in Nenagh, Carroll made a spur-of-the-moment decision to visit his home. He borrowed a bicycle and, under cover of darkness, made the 5-mile journey to his family farm. Unfortunately for Carroll, his parents had neighbours visiting at that time, one of whom was an active IRA member. Carroll was of particular interest to the IRA as he had been involved in the investigation into the Knocklong rescue of May 1919, and had recovered what was believed by the IRA to be 'incriminating evidence' during the search of the train from which Seán Hogan had been freed by Dan Breen and Seán Treacy. Several IRA Volunteers were in custody in February 1921, awaiting trial on charges connected with Knocklong, and Volunteer Martin Grace later recalled his belief that 'Carroll would be giving evidence at the trial'.[31]

Word was quickly sent to Commandant McDonnell and Captain Burke that Carroll was at home, and the following morning as he cycled back towards Nenagh he was taken captive. Captain Michael McCormack, a GHQ officer who was in the area at the time, was asked for instructions as to what should be done with Carroll. McCormack ordered that he be executed, and Carroll was shot dead at Ballycommon by a firing party of five men under the command of McDonnell.[32]

Several days later, Carroll's body was found at Ballyartella, about 5 miles outside Nenagh. He had been blindfolded, his hands were bound and he had been shot four times. Numerous notices were posted in the locality warning people not to attend the funeral of the dead constable. His father also received a letter warning him that if the police carried out reprisals in response to the killing, he and his remaining sons would be killed. It was subsequently reported that nobody from the local area attended the funeral.[33] Referring to Carroll's death as 'a murder of this constable by his own acquaintances', the county inspector urged that official reprisals be carried out, as they 'demonstrate the authority and power of a government ... but the action taken by way of reprisal has not been nearly drastic enough'.[34] Over twelve months later, his brother, Patrick, was shot dead on 13 June 1922, just before the Civil War began, and the family's farmhouse was burned down on the same night.

In February 1921 two former British soldiers from Templemore, James Maher and Patrick O'Meara, were abducted and executed. As was customary in such cases throughout Ireland, their bodies were left on the road with signs affixed reading, 'executed by IRA, spies and informers beware'.[35] The RIC reported that they had been executed on suspicion of being friendly with, or giving information to, the police. The county inspector stated this to be untrue, adding that 'these two men never gave any information ... and were absolutely useless to us'.[36] In reprisal for these deaths, two local men, Larry Hickey and William Loughnane, were shot dead in their homes in Thurles on that same evening and another man, Denis Regan, was badly wounded. The RIC categorised the three men as Sinn Féiners, and stated it was believed that they had been shot by 'friends of Maher and O'Meara'.[37]

In March 1921 Séamus Robinson, Officer Commanding the Third Tipperary Brigade, sent word to local commanders that each unit would have to become substantially more active.[38] The IRA in Cork city and county was under pressure from Crown forces, and to help alleviate the situation, it was ordered that a policeman or Black and Tan was to be shot in every town and village in Tipperary. The intention was to draw reinforcements into Tipperary and away from Cork. During March and April 1921 the RIC barracks at Dovea, Drombane, Holycross, Roskeen and Shevry were the subjects of continuous attacks by the IRA – to such an extent that they had to be evacuated. As soon as the police had withdrawn, the barracks were destroyed, to prevent their reoccupation. On 4 March 1921 Commandant Paddy Hogan of the second battalion arranged for a flying column to enter Cashel with the intention of carrying out Robinson's order. Information had been received that RIC Constable James Beasant was a frequent visitor to Cantwell's Bar.[39] Hogan entered the pub while Volunteer Tom Nagle stood guard outside because an RIC patrol was standing nearby. Hogan fired several shots at Beasant, but to no avail, as his ammunition was damp from being stored outdoors. Beasant and Hogan scuffled violently, and Nagle entered the bar when he heard the commotion inside. He shot the policeman once in the head, killing him instantly.[40] Miss Cantwell, the publican's daughter, was also badly wounded. Aged twenty-six, Constable Beasant was a former soldier from Wiltshire who had six months' RIC service and was employed as a driver in the transport section.

Beasant's death had dramatic consequences when the Volunteers involved left Cashel and dispersed to various safe houses. Hogan and another Volunteer, Patrick Keane, spent the night with the Dagg family at Derryclooney, and awoke the next morning to find the house surrounded by the military. Hogan told Keane that they were trapped and would have to fight for their lives, so both opened fire. During the exchange of shots that followed, Hogan was killed. Keane surrendered after the Dagg family implored him, 'in God's name or we will all be killed'. An officer who had been wounded in the encounter ordered a sergeant to shoot the prisoner if the convoy was fired upon while returning to Cahir Barracks. On the journey, the convoy was stopped by a party of Black and Tans who wanted to take custody of the prisoner, but the officer in charge refused to hand him over, stating that Keane was in military custody and they were responsible for him. Keane later believed that he had been fortunate to escape the clutches of the Black and Tans, as he might have suffered the fate of other captured IRA Volunteers who had been killed in custody. On arrival in Cahir he was placed in the custody of the military police, but feared that Auxiliaries who frequented the barracks 'in all stages of drunkenness and at all hours of the night' could cause him harm. While a concert was taking place in the barracks, Keane managed to knock out the one military policeman who was guarding him. He escaped by climbing out of the exercise yard and then scaling the perimeter wall of the barracks. He later rejoined his flying column, returning to what he described as a 'hero's welcome'.[41]

The introduction of flying columns to Tipperary put the RIC under additional pressure and, in response, County Inspector Gates suggested espousing IRA tactics by establishing several 'flying columns of military and police ... taking to the hills in pursuit', with the support of the Royal Air Force. He attributed the surge in violence to 'bands of armed men roaming the country' and repeated his erroneous belief that they were under the command of the 'notorious' Daniel Breen.[42] By this stage in the conflict, Breen was being linked with most killings and ambushes in Tipperary regardless of whether he actually took part or not. Gates believed that the community was 'sick of the situation' as they could see 'the ruin and misery' it entailed. However, he also asserted that the populace lacked moral courage, and that until the flying columns and their 'reign of terror' had been broken, there could be no hope of 'a sane and moderate public opinion'. He referenced ongoing disciplinary problems within the Black and Tans and Auxiliary Division, but claimed that morale was splendid and discipline 'rapidly improving as undesirable recruits are weeded out'.[43]

On 20 March 1921 Constable William Campbell was shot dead in the rear yard of Mullinahone Barracks after going outside to get coal from an outbuilding. A single man from Longford, Campbell had eight years' police service, having been a farmer prior to joining. Newspapers reported that he was shot from behind the wall of the barracks by unknown men, and County Inspector Gates stated his belief that the ambush was carried out by a party of rebels lying in wait.[44] Campbell's body was removed to Tipperary military barracks for an inquest, but it was not possible to form a jury because of intimidation. When the RIC barracks at Dovea, Drombane, Holycross, Roskeen and Shevry were evacuated during March and April 1921, the station parties were transferred to the heavily fortified garrison at Castlefogarty near Thurles. The IRA was reluctant to attack this garrison and Constable Harold Redvers Danton Browne, a Black and Tan stationed at Castlefogarty, wrote to his parents in England that his station was reputed to be 'the most comfortable, but one of the most dangerous in Ireland'.[45]

One of the most significant police deaths of the conflict occurred in April 1921, when District Inspector Gilbert Potter from Cahir was captured and executed by the IRA. Intelligence had been received that a military convoy passed twice a week between Cahir and Clogheen, and IRA Brigade Headquarters ordered a combined attack by flying columns from both the First and Second Brigades under the command of Dan Breen. They lay in wait on 23 April 1921 for several hours at Hyland's Cross, but the convoy did not arrive. An order was given to withdraw from the area due to a large military presence. As the IRA departed, a smaller column of soldiers carrying rations arrived unexpectedly and there was an exchange of shots, resulting in the death of one soldier and the wounding of several others. The remaining soldiers surrendered and were disarmed. As the ambush was unfolding, IRA scouts a short distance away stopped a car driving towards the scene and interrogated the male occupant, who was dressed in civilian clothing. He told the Volunteers that he was a doctor visiting patients, but when his car was searched a revolver was found. Volunteer Seán Downey recognised him as Gilbert Potter, the local RIC district inspector.[46]

Potter was taken prisoner and brought overnight with the flying column via the Knockmealdown Mountains into Waterford, stopping along the way at Mount Melleray Abbey. The group received a 'hearty welcome and meal from the monks'.[47] The monks knew that one of their guests was an IRA prisoner, but made no attempt to intervene. Knowing that there would be intense military activity when it was realised that Potter had been captured, the Volunteers took shelter in the Comeragh Mountains. Potter was held captive for several days while the IRA offered to exchange his life for that of Thomas Traynor, an IRA Volunteer who was awaiting execution in Mountjoy Prison for his involvement in an ambush on an Auxiliary Division patrol at Brunswick Street, Dublin on 14 March 1921, during which one Volunteer and two policemen had been killed. During his captivity, Potter established a rapport with his captors, which brought a rare element of humanity to an otherwise brutal conflict. The IRA hostage takers grew to like Potter, and some later recalled that he developed a respect and understanding for their aspiration to independence, while disagreeing strongly with the method they had chosen in pursuit of it.[48] One Volunteer guarding Potter later described him 'as undoubtedly a gentlemanly sort of fellow'.[49] Another recalled that he was 'a very nice kind of man and although fanatically attached to doing his duty ... he admired the adherence we showed to our duty as we saw it'. His captors believed that Potter had come to respect them for their 'sincere and honest purpose' in trying to achieve independence.[50]

It was quickly realised by the police that Potter was missing when his abandoned car was discovered near the scene of the ambush. The county inspector reported to Dublin Castle that Potter had been kidnapped, no trace of him had been discovered, and there was every reason to believe that he had been 'foully murdered'.[51] For the IRA, the mutual respect and liking that had grown between captor and captive made it 'very embarrassing' to have to consider executing him if ordered to do so.[52] While waiting for news about the fate of Thomas Traynor, in a notable gesture of humanity, his captors put a proposal to Potter that they would allow him to escape if he gave his word of honour that he would take no further action against them. Potter expressed his appreciation for the gesture, but stated that he could not give his word, as he 'must do his duty as he saw it'. Battalion intelligence officer Thomas Carew came to where Potter was being held captive and stated that he would wait with them until the *Evening Herald* newspaper arrived, as it was expected to carry news about Traynor. Some time after 9 p.m. on 27 April, the paper arrived and the headline read 'Thomas Traynor hanged this morning'. Carew remarked 'I am sorry for you, Potter,' before leaving.

A firing squad was assembled under Commandant Dinny Lacey, who chose Volunteers Allen and Crowe to carry out the execution, as both wanted revenge for the deaths of their brothers at the hands of Crown forces. A grave had been dug, and Potter was forced to stand in it as the Volunteers took aim and fired at him, causing non-fatal injuries. Potter cried out, 'I am not dead,' so Commandant Lacey stepped forward and administered a fatal shot to the head. On 8 May 1921 his wife, Mrs Lily Potter, received a package with a Cahir postmark containing her husband's diary, will, signet ring, watch and poignant final letter to her and their four children. In this letter, Potter wrote: 'I request those in authority with IRA to send to my wife my note book which contains messages for her … there are, I am sure, humane leaders who will pity a wife who is Irish, as I am also.' The package was accompanied by a letter signed 'Officer Commanding IRA', stating that 'DI Potter, having been legally arrested and tried, was sentenced to death, which was carried out on Wednesday, 27th April'.[53] Mrs Potter collapsed on receiving the news.

Newspapers reported that Potter, who had served for twenty-one years in the RIC, was stationed in Cahir for a number of years and was 'very popular, having done much to keep the town quiet'.[54] Following his death, ten farms in the locality were badly damaged in reprisal attacks, including Tincurry House near Cahir, where the Soloheadbeg ambushers had hidden following the ambush of 21 January 1919. A notice stating that the reprisals were officially sanctioned appeared in local newspapers, confirming that the colonel commanding the 16th Infantry Brigade had ordered that fourteen homes be destroyed on the grounds that 'the persons concerned are active supporters of armed rebels and that they reside in the area'.[55] Several months after the Truce, and at the request of Mrs Potter, the IRA disinterred her husband's body, as her claim for compensation and insurance could not proceed without proof of his death, and the Potter family wanted to give him a Christian burial.[56] His funeral took place in Clonmel on 30 August 1921. In his last diary entry, Potter wrote that he was to be 'executed this evening at 7 p.m. … my guardians are not at all anxious to kill me, but have received orders from GHQ which they cannot disobey'.[57]

The breakdown in Volunteer discipline that had taken place during Potter's detention and execution did not go unnoticed, and became an issue of concern for IRA commanders. A short time after his death, an ambush was planned in the same area for a joint military and RIC convoy that was expected to pass. Dinny Lacey, commander of the flying column, commented that he expected an RIC district inspector to be among the convoy. Volunteer Andrew Kennedy remarked 'if there is a district inspector we had better shoot him when we get him and not be crying about it afterwards'. Lacey apparently took exception to this frivolous remark, and Kennedy later recalled that he was punished for it by being selected for some 'tough assignments'.[58]

In April 1921 IRA brigade headquarters issued an instruction that bridges in each battalion area were to be demolished. The previous practice of trenching roads had been largely overcome by military patrols carrying wooden planks, which were then used as improvised bridges, on their Crossley or Lancia tenders. On 27 April Volunteers from Cappawhite in south Tipperary destroyed a bridge at Ballymore that was used by military and police convoys travelling between Tipperary town and Dundrum. Two IRA members, Lieutenant Martin Purcell and Volunteer Patrick Maher, were captured during follow-up raids and taken into military custody in Tipperary Barracks. Maher was transferred to the Curragh military hospital in Kildare, where he subsequently died, and Purcell died while in custody in Tipperary. Believing that Purcell had been murdered, the IRA set out to exact retribution. They had valuable sources of accurate intelligence, as two RIC sergeants in Annacarty and Dundrum were sympathetic to the Volunteers, providing them with ciphers and other important information.[59]

On 6 May 1921 a patrol of policemen travelling along a rural road, approaching the Anglican Church at Annacarty, observed several men, one of whom was equipped with field glasses, in the vicinity of a nearby farmhouse. Shots were fired at the policemen, who hastily retreated towards their barracks. As they withdrew from the area, they encountered a civilian, who was taken prisoner as they suspected him to be a member of the ambush party. As they reached the main road, they came under heavy and sustained fire, resulting in the deaths of Sergeant James Kingston and his civilian prisoner. The remaining members of the party escaped injury, and the ambushers swiftly left the area. A native of Clonakilty in County Cork, Sergeant Kingston had twenty-six years' RIC service and was married with six children. Following his death, fairs and markets in the Cappawhite area were prohibited, and the farmhouse near the scene of the ambush was set ablaze. In his report the county inspector described the dead civilian as an 'unknown ambusher'.[60] In an effort to identify the man, the RIC took the unusual step of photographing the body and displaying it in various shops in the locality, but nobody came forward to claim the remains.[61]

In late April 1921 Commandant Seán Gaynor, along with officers from every other county in Ireland, was summoned to a meeting at IRA GHQ in Dublin. One of the issues addressed by IRA Chief of Staff Richard Mulcahy was the allegation that some brigades were not pulling their weight.[62] On his return to Tipperary, Gaynor selected the IRA in Newport for restructuring, as he believed them to be particularly in need of reform. He targeted District Inspector Harold Biggs, an exceptionally unpopular man even by the standards of the time, as a priority. Biggs had arrived in Tipperary in August 1920 as a member of the Auxiliary Division, but he had later transferred into the regular RIC and become district inspector for Newport. The barracks in Newport had been evacuated, but a heavily fortified garrison was established at Rosehill House just outside the town. Biggs quickly established a reputation for aggression, with one IRA Volunteer remembering him as 'truculent and active' – a bitter opponent of the IRA, with few equals.[63] On one occasion, it was alleged, Biggs went to Silvermines village after Sunday Mass and forced Mass-goers to sing 'God Save the King' at gunpoint. For local IRA commanders, the death of Biggs, described by Gaynor as 'a vicious Black and Tan', became a priority. If he were killed, it would send an unambiguous signal to other policemen about the dangers of active aggression. It would also remove the perception that IRA members in the district of Newport had been deficient in conducting military operations.

On 15 May 1921 brigade officers met at a house in Newport to plan how they might assassinate Biggs. During the meeting, a scout told them that Biggs had just passed by in a car with three other people, all in civilian clothing. It was believed that the party was going to visit the house of a local landowner, Major Gabbitt, who regularly entertained Biggs along with other RIC and military officers. Plans were quickly made to ambush the car when it left Gabbitt's house for the return journey to Newport. Twelve Volunteers assembled, and the two possible routes that the party could take from the house were covered. After several hours the car was seen leaving the house and as it approached the townland of Coolboreen, the IRA opened fire. The car travelled on for about 20 yards before it stopped, and three of the occupants got out and ran away. A Volunteer recognised Biggs and shouted 'That's the DI,' prompting the IRA to open fire again. Biggs was shot dead, another person was badly wounded and a third managed to return fire before escaping. Gabbitt, who was driving the car, emerged with his hands raised, shouting 'Stop, stop, there is a lady in the car!'[64] He told the Volunteers that a Miss Winifred Barrington had been shot and that another female, Miss Ryan, was also in the car. While she was physically unscathed, Miss Ryan gave Gaynor and the other IRA members 'dog's abuse' for having shot Miss Barrington. Another member of the ambush party, Paddy Ryan Lacken, silenced her, saying 'It served them right, and only for the bitch being in bad company, she would not be shot.'[65] The IRA party then quickly left the area, as they expected an influx of reinforcements and reprisals following the shootings.

The death of Winifred Barrington attracted significant attention, given that she was not only a female civilian, but also the daughter of Sir Charles Barrington of Glenstal Castle in County Limerick. Several similar incidents had taken place since the outbreak of hostilities, including one at Gort in County Galway, when a car containing military officers in civilian attire and their female companions was ambushed, resulting in the death of Mrs Blake, the wife of the local county inspector. Such incidents provoked great controversy, with the press calling the death of female civilians 'deplorable events', but blame was attributed to individual soldiers and policemen for putting female civilians in harm's way in the first place. *The Times* editorialised that if officers permitted ladies to accompany them, they were 'directly responsible for any harm that may unhappily befall them in the event of an attack. That is the rule of all wars.'[66] Shortly afterwards, a military court of enquiry took place in Limerick into the deaths of District Inspector Biggs and Miss Barrington. Miss Ryan, who had escaped injury during the ambush, gave evidence that the IRA Volunteers fired several shots into the body of Biggs as he lay on the road, with one of them remarking that Biggs was 'the man we wanted'.[67]

On 15 May 1921 a party of policemen was attacked in the village of Bansha as they left Mass. Approximately 30 yards from the church, a group of IRA Volunteers opened fire from behind cover, hitting three of the policemen. Constable John Nutley was killed instantly, while Sergeant Sullivan was seriously wounded and Constable McLoughlin received slight injuries.[68] Nutley, a single 22-year-old from Galway, had been in the RIC for only twelve months, having previously been a soldier and a labourer.[69] Several houses, including that of local publican Mrs O'Dwyer, were destroyed in reprisal.[70] On the following Sunday the parish priest, Father Byrne, referred in his sermon to recent events. He asked parishioners to pray for the dead and wounded, and also for those who had lost their property or homes. He ended by saying that 'no words can describe the appalling condition of the parish', and expressing his hope that future Sabbaths would not be desecrated by similar events.[71] The county inspector reported that retaliations carried out in respect of Nutley's death were 'official reprisals'.[72]

The Auxiliary Division was regarded by the IRA as its greatest threat, but, in common with the Black and Tans, indiscipline and drunkenness among its ranks played into the hands of the Volunteers and of well-placed critics of British government policy in Ireland. The Labour Party Commission of Enquiry, for example, concluded that the Auxiliaries did not seem to recognise the authority of Dublin Castle and questioned whom they served.[73] One notorious incident occurred on 17 April 1921 at Castleconnell, County Limerick, close to the border with Tipperary. Three off-duty Auxiliaries in plain clothes were drinking in a hotel when it was raided by other Auxiliaries, also in plain clothes. Each group mistook the other for IRA members and opened fire. When the exchange of shots ended, an RIC sergeant, a temporary cadet and the hotel manager, Denis O'Donovan, had all been killed.[74] At the subsequent military enquiry, the deputy adjutant general commented that the Auxiliaries 'had the wind up, blood up, and did what they used to do in the trenches in France'. He pleaded that in such circumstances they should not be held criminally responsible, but asserted that they were 'not fit to be policemen, nor were any Auxiliaries'.[75]

In a significant development in May 1921, the Auxiliary Division completely withdrew from north Tipperary in order to reinforce companies based elsewhere in Ireland. Commandant Seán Scott in Templemore received a message from Michael Collins stating that B Company was about to vacate Templemore Abbey, the home of Sir John Carden, which had been commandeered in 1920. Collins directed that it must be destroyed 'at all costs ... even at the loss of men'.[76] Scott was surprised to learn that the abbey was to be vacated, as he had no local intelligence to that effect. Because of the confidence he had in Collins, however, preparations were made to burn the mansion as ordered. The abbey had been formidably fortified by the Auxiliaries, and was an important symbolic target for the local Volunteers as it was the ancestral seat of the Carden family, who had been notoriously unpopular landlords in the Templemore area during the Great Famine.[77] Scott's faith in the information supplied by Collins was justified. Shortly after he had received his orders, and much to the relief of the Volunteers lying in wait, the Auxiliaries were seen loading their transports and leaving the abbey. That night, a party of IRA Volunteers seized 30 gallons of petrol from various businesses in the town and broke into the mansion. It was ineptly set ablaze, however, and some Volunteers received burns and other injuries in the process. Within a few hours the elaborate Gothic Revival mansion and its outbuildings had been razed. The destruction of the abbey and the swift departure of the Auxiliaries may not have been a military victory for the IRA, but these events were powerfully symbolic.

In June 1921 the already fraught situation of RIC members in Tipperary further deteriorated. The north county inspector reported that the number of outrages – encompassing deaths, robbery of mail, intimidation and boycotting – had risen from fifty-four in May to eighty in June. In the south riding, the county inspector reported that the situation was so bad 'that it could not get any worse'. Long periods confined to barracks and the constant threat of bodily harm had a devastating effect on both the physical and mental wellbeing of policemen. The situation was particularly difficult for those who had the additional burden of worrying about friends and family suffering intimidation and boycotting. It was noticeable that morale varied substantially between different barracks, and this was remarked upon by the county inspector for the north riding. He noted that in strong stations, from which good fighting patrols could be sent out, morale was good, but in smaller stations, where men were doing nothing but holding their post, 'it is only natural to find pessimism and a fed up attitude ... the men naturally want to hunt for the rebel, and they want to see the government give a free hand to those charged with settling the country'.[78]

The most violent incident to take place in Tipperary during this period occurred on Friday 3 June 1921, when four policemen were killed and another four were seriously wounded in an ambush at Modreeny, between Borrisokane and Cloughjordan. Commandant Seán Gaynor planned the ambush after receiving information from an RIC constable based in Borrisokane. Up to thirteen policemen were scheduled to make their way by bicycle from Borrisokane to Cloughjordan that morning to attend the Petty Sessions Court.[79] Gaynor planned an ambush at the midway point between the two towns. The location was chosen because it was remote, distant from possible reinforcements, and at a bend in the road surrounded by high ground. This gave the attackers a significant tactical advantage. IRA reinforcements were brought into the area, but Gaynor did not reveal the intended target until the last minute. As his information had come from a policeman, he could not be certain that it was accurate and he had to consider the possibility of being lured into a trap. A group of more than twenty Volunteers – a flying column, assisted by the Cloughjordan Volunteers – took part in the ambush. Just before they set out for the ambush site at 4 a.m. on 3 June, the Volunteers were briefed as to their intended target. Most were armed with shotguns; several had rifles, while some of the officers had revolvers.

When they reached Modreeny, the Volunteers concealed themselves and waited. The brigade had been practising semaphore in previous months, and this skill proved beneficial when, at 9 a.m., a scout used it to signal that the policemen were approaching. The signal also caused surprise, however, when it revealed that instead of the thirteen policemen they had anticipated, the convoy actually consisted of over forty policemen and soldiers. Despite the increased odds, the IRA commander decided to attack, and blew a whistle as a signal to open fire. The leading military lorry was not hit and quickly left the scene, thus ensuring that reinforcements would be called. The next lorry, containing five policemen, was then attacked. Constable James Briggs died instantly and eight other policemen were badly wounded. The ambush took a bizarre turn when IRA Commander Paddy Kennedy was seen firing at the police with a shotgun at close range while his rosary beads hung around his neck.[80]

After thirty minutes the IRA ceased firing, knowing that reinforcements would soon arrive from Nenagh, 7 miles away. Before withdrawing, they took several weapons and substantial amounts of ammunition from the bodies of the dead and wounded policemen. Medical assistance was given by the local GP, Doctor Quigley, and the local priest, Father Smith, administered the last rites to the dead and injured. Three of the wounded policemen, constables John Cantlon, Martin Feeney and William Walsh, died the following day.[81] A single man from Scotland, Constable Briggs had joined the RIC in 1920, and had been awarded the Military Medal and Distinguished Conduct Medal during the Great War. His memoriam card contained some poignant verses written by his mother, including: 'Lord, teach me to live that when my life is ended, I'll be met at the gates by my dear hero son.' The Modreeny ambush was considered a significant victory by the IRA, given the number of casualties inflicted on the police and the fact that no IRA members were wounded. A letter of commendation was sent to Commandant Gaynor by IRA Chief of Staff Richard Mulcahy.

On 28 June 1921 the last large-scale operation against Crown forces in north Tipperary took place when Borrisoleigh Barracks was attacked. The barracks was of strategic importance as it was located on the main street of the village, on the main road between Nenagh and Thurles, and close to the large garrison town of Templemore. The barracks had been heavily fortified during the latter part of 1920. Steel shutters had been placed on all doors and windows, and sandbags and barbed wire surrounded the perimeter. The plan was to employ the same tactics as had been used in previous attacks on terraced barracks, like those at Kilcommon and Rearcross: after gaining access to the roof of the barracks via adjacent premises, the Volunteers would remove the slates, pour petrol into the void, and set the barracks on fire, forcing the police to abandon it. The IRA received intelligence, however, that the upstairs of Maher's public house, next door to Borrisoleigh Barracks, had been sealed off by the police and booby traps had been laid. It was necessary, therefore, to adopt new tactics. Local IRA Commander Jim Stapleton decided to use one of the rudimentary 'allowee' bombs commonly used by the IRA. These were manufactured by taking a stick of gelignite and wrapping it in a coating of sticky local mud. The fuse was lit and the bomb, if thrown accurately, would stick to the building before detonating. In the days leading up to the attack, over thirty Volunteers were assigned to the manufacture of such bombs. Up to 400 IRA men from all three Tipperary brigades took part in the attack itself.

On the evening of the attack, all roads leading into Borrisoleigh were barricaded, trenches were dug and telephone wires were cut. Parties of Volunteers lay in wait at various locations, as it was expected that reinforcements would be summoned by the Borrisoleigh garrison when the attack started. Diversionary sniper attacks were planned for police stations at Gurtaderrybeg, Templetouhy and Barnane. The main attack began at 11 p.m. when rifle fire was directed at the barracks and the bombs were thrown. The barracks soon caught fire, but the flames quickly died out. More bombs were thrown, with similar results, and Stapleton realised that the barracks was not going to be set ablaze easily. The police inside the barracks sent up flares to summon assistance from Templemore; but none was forthcoming as it was feared that reinforcements would be lured into an ambush. As dawn approached IRA commanders decided to call an end the attack, using a prearranged signal – the ringing of the bell in the Roman Catholic church. The signal had been deliberately chosen by Jim Stapleton to cause annoyance to the local parish priest, a vocal opponent of the IRA.[82]

In the period leading up to this attack, farm labourer and ex-soldier Patrick Meagher was executed by the IRA because he had been seen socialising with policemen and he had ignored warnings to stop. His body was found by early-morning Mass-goers. The usual notice of 'Executed by the IRA, spies and informers beware' was affixed to his corpse.[83] Two days later 21-year-old Constable Joseph Bourke, a former soldier from Cork who had joined the police in 1920, was shot dead while standing at the door of Templemore Barracks. The exact circumstances of his death were not released by official sources.[84] However, one newspaper reported that RIC Constable William Sheehan had been arrested and was in custody at the military barracks in Templemore in connection with Bourke's death.[85] In August 1921 a court martial took place at Victoria Barracks in Cork, at which Sheehan was charged with the 'wilful murder' of Bourke. Medical evidence was given that Sheehan had a 'delusion of persecution' and that he had told doctors that he was being 'tormented by everybody'. The court martial accepted that Sheehan was unable to stand trial due to insanity, and he was remanded in custody to be dealt with according to military regulations.[86] He was subsequently committed to Broadmoor Asylum in England.[87]

The last member of the RIC in County Tipperary to be killed before the Truce came into effect on 11 July 1921 was Joseph Shelsher from London, a former soldier stationed at Bansha, who had been in the RIC for less than twelve months. On the evening of 1 July he left his barracks at about 9 p.m. Two hours later, his body was found on a nearby road by a passing labourer.[88] He had been shot once in the head, and his revolver and ammunition had been taken.[89] Following his death, a large number of police and military reinforcements came into the area from the garrison in Tipperary town. Most business premises in Tipperary town and Bansha were ordered by the military to close for periods ranging from several hours to several days as a mark of respect to the deceased.

The long memory and equally lengthy reach of the IRA were powerfully demonstrated on 7 July 1921, when the body of a retired RIC sergeant, Anthony Foody, was found at Carralavin, County Mayo, by a local postman. He had been shot dead, and around his neck was a notice reading 'Revenge for Dwyer and the Ragg'.[90] Foody had retired from the RIC only three weeks earlier and had purchased land at Bonniconlon, near to where his body was found. It was later established that Foody had been taken at gunpoint by two armed and masked men from the house of a cousin he was visiting.[91] It was reported that two men related to him had been arrested in connection with his death, but no charges were ever preferred.[92] Foody had served in Thurles before retiring and was believed by Tipperary IRA members to have been responsible for the deaths of IRA Volunteers James McCarthy and Tom Dwyer in the 'Ragg incident' of 4 March 1920. McCarthy and Dwyer were shot dead in their homes by masked men as a reprisal for the shooting of two uniformed RIC constables in Fanning's public house at The Ragg, near Thurles. The IRA claimed that the men who shot them were policemen in disguise. Foody became a marked man following this incident, and had a narrow escape on 31 May 1920, when three armed and masked men called to his house and quizzed his wife as to his whereabouts. Stating that they were 'Irish police' who had to do their 'duty', they searched the house, but left when they realised that Foody was not at home.

On 4 April 1920 Foody went to Dovea church with eight other policemen to attend Mass, and found that a pew that had been paid for and used by RIC members for many years had been destroyed and left outside the church. Many churches in Ireland had pews that had been funded by the local RIC or donated for the RIC's use by benefactors; some dated back to the Famine era. As the conflict progressed, it became common for such pews to be removed from churches, or even destroyed. Considerable pressure was placed upon the clergy and the general population to uphold the policy of boycott and intimidation of the RIC; while Foody complained to the local parish priest about the removal of the pew, it was to no avail. The saga of 'the peelers' pew' was even incorporated into a ballad, with the lyrics 'it burnt like the trees ... 'twas nice timber for the fire'.[93] Local IRA Volunteers berated Foody and the other policemen as they left the church, with one remarking, 'We won't have your breath amongst us.'[94] Foody had been fortunate to escape death while serving in Tipperary, but even his retirement and relocation to a different part of Ireland were not enough to ensure his survival.

In 1921, the Tipperary IRA believed that a police 'murder gang' existed in the county, under the command of Head Constable Eugene Igoe from Thurles, who was well known to local Volunteers, having previously served in Shevry and Littleton. Prior to 'the Ragg incident', however, the IRA had regarded him to be 'an inoffensive man ... whose only interest was a buxom barmaid in a local pub'. In October 1920 a friendly policeman gave Commandant Jimmy Leahy a list of twelve names of prominent local people who had allegedly been targeted for assassination by the RIC. Leahy was surprised to see that the list contained not only his own name but also that of the Archbishop of Cashel, Dr John Mary Harty.[95] In January 1921 Igoe was transferred to Dublin as part of a reorganisation of the intelligence service under the command of Colonel Ormonde Winter (codename 'O'). It had been realised that the key to success against the IRA was accurate intelligence. Many IRA activists had relocated to Dublin to evade capture, and to counter this, a detachment of specially selected policemen with extensive local knowledge, drawn from different parts of Ireland, was formed under the command of Igoe, who was promoted by Winter to the rank of temporary head constable.[96] This 'identification company' patrolled the streets of Dublin in civilian attire looking for wanted men, and was a direct threat to 'the squad' that had been assembled by Michael Collins to carry out assassinations at his behest. Labelled 'the Igoe gang' by the IRA, this unit was intended to play the Volunteers at their own game.

Igoe was renowned for having an aggressive attitude. One of his superiors admitted that 'he needed to be handier with his gun than the gunmen were with theirs'. While the police in Dublin were full of admiration for Igoe, he was regarded by the IRA as a murderer. Thus, his life was in danger wherever he went. At the request of Michael Collins, Jimmy Leahy sent two Volunteers to Dublin with the intention of identifying Igoe for 'the squad'. They managed to do so, but, much to Leahy's regret, Igoe survived the conflict and went on to take part in secret service operations for the British government in other countries. He was unable to return to his farm in Mayo, however, for fear of reprisal. After the conflict had ended in 1922 and the RIC was in the process of being disbanded, Winter interceded on Igoe's behalf, recommending that his pension should be increased for his 'many services to the Crown in Ireland and elsewhere'.[97]

After two years marked by animosity and extreme bitterness on both sides, the conflict was approaching a finality of sorts. During the first half of 1921, informal negotiations aimed at brokering a ceasefire took place between the British government and representatives of the IRA. Patrick Clune, Archbishop of Perth in Western Australia, acted as an intermediary. The ongoing contact between Clune and Collins caused an exasperated Mark Sturgis, Assistant Under-Secretary at Dublin Castle, to comment in his diary, 'I wonder how it is that the archbishop sees Collins apparently without difficulty in Dublin, yet our intelligence fails to find him after weeks of searching'.[98] Another important negotiator in the peace process was General Jan Smuts, Prime Minister of South Africa. During the Boer War of 1899–1902, Smuts fought against the British and demonstrated a particular talent for guerrilla warfare, giving him credibility with Irish militants. On 22 June 1921 King George V opened a session of Parliament in Belfast, with a speech that is believed to have been an endorsement of the British government by publicly endorsing their attempts to make peace. The timing of the King's speech was critical, as martial law was due to be extended to the remaining counties of Ireland on 14 July. Events moved swiftly and on 28 June, Dublin Castle ordered the suspension of 'raids on premises frequented by persons of political importance'.[99] A Dáil peace conference began at the Mansion House in Dublin on 5 July, at which a tentative agreement was reached to the overtures of the British government, and a truce came into effect on Monday 11 July 1921.

For thousands of policemen who had survived the conflict, their relief at a ceasefire was tempered with apprehension, as they faced an uncertain future. In north Tipperary the county inspector reported that the men under his command did not receive the announcement of the Truce with acclaim, and that it was only natural, having suffered so much at the hands of 'known murderers', that they felt it difficult to restrain themselves when orders to carry out the Truce were received.[100] Despite the animosity that existed between the participants in the conflict, the Truce was reasonably well observed in practice, with liaison officers nominated on both sides to ensure that any breaches were dealt with swiftly. The inspector general of the RIC noted with some satisfaction that a 'tremendous weight' had been lifted from the civilian population, and that they were beginning to enjoy the benefits of peace.[101] Patrick Shea, the son of a serving RIC sergeant who had come through unhurt, expressed the relief of many police families: 'I would no longer lie in bed praying for the sound of his footsteps or watch the colour leave my mother's face when there was a knock on the door. Whatever the future might hold, fear had been banished.'[102]

4

The 'Unemployable Period': Truce, Treaty and Disbandment

> 'I never expected to see the day when ships would sail away to England with the Auxiliaries and the Black and Tans, the RIC and the British soldiery ... Dublin Castle itself – that dread Bastille of Ireland – formally surrendered into my hands'.
>
> Michael Collins[1]

The Truce commenced at noon on Monday 11 July 1921, and initially brought a degree of calm to a country ravaged by conflict. It was an uneasy peace, however, and both sides stood in readiness to resume hostilities should the Truce collapse. The agreement stated that the British government would not send further reinforcements to Ireland, and also that the military, RIC and Auxiliary Division would not engage in what were termed 'provocative' displays of militarism. It was also agreed that Volunteers would not be pursued or their military equipment seized. The IRA, which was now referred to as the 'Irish army' in official correspondence for the first time, undertook to cease all attacks on Crown forces and refrain from 'reciprocal confrontational displays'.[2] The campaign of boycotting and intimidation against the RIC

Disbandment parade of the RIC at the RIC Depot, Phoenix Park, 4 April 1922. The parade is being cheered by their comrades while a detachment of the Royal Artillery present arms. In keeping with RIC tradition, rifles are carried in the style known as the 'long trail'. *(Courtesy Police Museum, Belfast)*

and their families and those associated with them continued, however, albeit on a lesser scale.

Breaches of the Truce occurred on both sides, but political expediency ensured that most were overlooked. When they did occur, the allocation of blame presented difficulty for both sides, and had profound implications for the peace negotiations. One incident occurred in Tipperary on 10 November 1921, when two constables cycling from their barracks in Portroe village towards Nenagh were shot at. One was badly wounded, and Chief Secretary Hamar Greenwood told the House of Commons of his belief that 'the outrage was deliberately planned ... but there was no reason to suppose that the miscreants were other than irresponsible mischief-makers acting on their own initiative'. Greenwood stated that the matter was under investigation by the police in conjunction with the local Sinn Féin liaison officer.[3]

While relieved at the lull in hostilities, policemen were also frustrated at the terms of the Truce. The IRA was now formally recognised and acknowledged, giving the movement the status it sought. The RIC Deputy Inspector General, Charles Walsh, warned the force that extremists 'may commit serious breaches of the Truce ... but responsible Sinn Féin leaders now have a direct and immediate common interest with the British government in maintaining law and order'.[4] IRA members began to appear in public wearing military uniforms. In Tipperary, the county inspector reported on apparent breaches of the Truce that saw 'well-known murderers of police parading at will in front of the comrades of those who have been murdered'.[5] The movement took full advantage of the opportunity to recruit, drill and train. New recruits, who swelled the ranks of the Volunteers during the Truce period, were contemptuously referred to by some veteran members as 'truciliers'. Piaras Béaslaí categorised them as 'truce heroes' and noted that many were more aggressive and militant than those who had actually taken part in the campaign.[6] On 1 October 1921, Sir Nevil Macready, Commander-in-Chief of Crown forces in Ireland, cautioned the government that advantage had been taken of the Truce to convert the IRA, which three months previously had been little more than 'a disorganised rabble', into 'a well-disciplined, well-organized and well-armed force'.[7] The IRA ensured that it was ready to resume the conflict in earnest should the Truce collapse, while policemen confined to barracks could only watch and wait for the next phase of the political process.

At 2.30 a.m. on 6 December 1921, after prolonged negotiations, a treaty was signed by representatives of the British government led by Prime Minister Lloyd George and Colonial Secretary Winston Churchill and an Irish delegation including Michael Collins, Arthur Griffith and Cathal Brugha. The consequent transition to a new entity known as the Irish Free State had a profound effect on those serving in the administration of the state at the time. Their fate was referred to in Article 10 of the Treaty. It specified that compensation was to be paid to judges, officials, members of police forces and other public servants who were discharged or forced to retire due to the change of government. Expanding on this provision, Article 10 went on to state that the agreement would not apply to members of the Auxiliary Division or Black and Tans recruited in England during the previous two years, and that the British government would take responsibility for 'compensation or pensions as might be payable to such exempted persons'.[8] Article 10 of the Treaty therefore clearly distinguished between members of the RIC who had been serving prior to 1919, and those who had been recruited since the conflict began. For Irish policemen who had been linked by association with the activities of the Black and Tans and Auxiliaries, it was an important distinction. Article 10 also clearly demonstrated the intention of the signatories to leave the pre-1919 RIC intact, and that these men would form the core of new police forces to be established in both northern and southern Ireland. The stipulation also adhered to the terms of the Government of Ireland Act, 1920, which intended to establish new parliaments in both jurisdictions.

When details of the Treaty became known, they were received with disappointment by the RIC. In a memo to cabinet on 10 December 1921, Greenwood revealed that the peace agreement with Sinn Féin had 'aroused the liveliest feeling of apprehension in all ranks of the constabulary' and that it was their unanimous opinion that the whole force should be disbanded rather than being subdivided and handed over to the governments of northern and southern Ireland. Greenwood stated that the RIC had been 'an imperial force at the time they joined it, and its former members had no desire to serve in any part of it if it ceased to be so'.[9] For career policemen such as Limerick County Inspector John Regan, the distinction between Irishmen who served in the RIC before 1919 and men recruited in Great Britain as the conflict escalated was also of significance. In his memoir, he made the salient point that the Black and Tans 'could return to their native land after the conflict ended, but many former members of the RIC could not remain in theirs'.[10]

An intensive campaign of lobbying by representative bodies for all ranks within the force began, which included sending telegrams to both the Prime Minister and the King. A deputation travelled to London to lobby Churchill and other Members of Parliament personally. The delegation of over twenty rank-and-file members was led by County Inspector Gregory, Chairman of the Officers' Representative Body.[11] They engaged the leading Dublin barrister Timothy Healy KC as their senior counsel.[12] The *Constabulary Gazette* editorialised that 'the force is unsettled and discontent rife ... because of the uncertainty of the future'. Greenwood had several meetings with the representatives and their legal advisors, who expressed 'utmost disfavour' at the possibility of being handed over to the government of the new Irish Free State. Their main objection was that the new government would be 'composed entirely of members of Sinn Féin, against whom all their efforts had been directed during the recent struggle'. Representatives also emphasised their belief that it would not be possible for many policemen to return to their homes, and that while they may not face physical danger, 'their lives could be made intolerable by the hostility of their neighbours'.[13] Greenwood offered no assurance to the representatives that their demands for complete disbandment would be met, but he undertook to consider the proposal and submit it to the cabinet.

Aside from the sensitive political considerations, Greenwood was conscious of the serious financial implications of completely disbanding the RIC, a measure for which a budget had not been allocated. Article 10 of the Treaty stated that the cost of disbanding the post-1919 force, which numbered some 5,796 men of constable and sergeant ranks, would be borne by the British government. If the 6,571 men who had joined before 1919 were also to be disbanded on the same terms, substantial additional costs would be incurred. On 17 December 1921 Greenwood sent a memo to all police barracks, reassuring policemen that the British government was fully conscious of its obligation towards those who had been, and would shortly cease to be, servants of the state. He went on to say that the unique position of the force required special treatment, but that justice would be done 'to members of that gallant force ... His Majesty's Government will be the ultimate guarantor of their payments and pensions'.[14] At a cabinet meeting on 12 December 1921 the issue of complete disbandment was again discussed, and it was agreed that the government 'must assure just treatment to members of the RIC', but full disbandment was not conceded, and Greenwood was instructed to submit a memorandum to cabinet.[15]

By January 1922 the matter had finally been determined, and the Provisional Government of Ireland Committee, under the chairmanship of Winston Churchill, submitted its recommendations to the cabinet. Commenting on the logistics of British withdrawal from Ireland, Churchill described the issue of policing as 'the most difficult question of all'. Article 10 of the Treaty had contemplated the transfer of the old RIC to the Irish provisional government, but the attitude adopted by members of the force made it clear that such a transfer, even if it could be managed, would not be in the interests of the new government. Churchill recommended that the RIC should be completely disbanded as soon as practicable, as former members might want to enlist in the new police forces to be established. Such recruitment would provide technical experience to the new forces and lessen the burden of compensation on the British government.[16] A sub-committee established to examine the issue of compensation estimated the annual cost of pensioning off all eligible permanent RIC members to be £1,312,448. There would be an additional cost of £230,000 per annum to compensate members recruited in England after 1919. The committee recommended that the government of the Irish Free State should not be 'saddled with this liability' in the interests of adhering to the spirit of Article 10 of the Treaty. An assumption was also made in the report that the Irish Free State would, in due course, assume financial responsibility for RIC pensions. The representative bodies strongly objected to this proposal as 'the whereabouts of former RIC members would then be fully known to the Irish Free State'.[17]

Since the RIC had effectively ceased to function as a civil police force, a policing vacuum existed throughout Ireland. The constabulary abandoned its barracks and petty sessions courts stopped operating. In June 1921 an alternative system of justice was established by the IRA, which consisted of Sinn Féin courts and the Republican Police. Usurping the RIC allowed the Volunteer movement to assert its authority over the community while at the same time challenging the power of the state.[18] Michael Collins did not believe, however, that the Republican Police was suitable to be retained as a replacement organisation for the RIC. Writing to W. T. Cosgrave, Minister for Local Government, Collins said that he did not want a 'casual police force without proper training ... it is not necessary for me to illustrate this by pointing to the wretched Republican Police system and to the awful personnel'.[19]

The task of founding, recruiting, training and deploying a new police force was an onerous one. Following the Truce of July 1921 and subsequent Anglo-Irish Treaty of December 1921, bitter and divisive debates took place in the Dáil. On 7 January 1922 the Treaty was ratified by a small margin of sixty-four votes to fifty-seven. The refusal by a significant section of Sinn Féin and the IRA to accept this vote ensured that Ireland moved inexorably towards Civil War. On 9 February 1922 the inaugural meeting of a committee tasked by the provisional government with establishing a new police force took place at the Gresham Hotel in Dublin. Michael Collins was present, as were Michael Staines, who would become the first commissioner of the new force, Eamonn Duggan, IRA Director of Intelligence, and IRA Chief of Staff Eoin O'Duffy, who would become the force's second commissioner. Despite the contempt displayed for the RIC by militant nationalists during the previous three years, of the nine men invited by Collins to manage the new police force, seven had previously served in the RIC. Thirteen of the twenty committee members were either serving or former members of the force, with a further three coming from the Dublin Metropolitan Police.[20] The new force was initially named the Civic Guard, and Collins requested of Churchill that demobilisation of the RIC be delayed to give sufficient time for the Civic Guard to be established.[21] The task of formally disbanding the RIC began in earnest, however, and operated in parallel with the efforts of the new Irish government to find men to replace them.[22]

On 5 March 1922 Collins made the first public reference to the new Civic Guard during a speech at College Green in Dublin. He stated that he wanted 'the support of the people for the new police we are forming ... it will be a people's guard for the protection of all classes and parties'. The organising committee for the Civic Guard recommended that the force should have a strength of 4,300 men, under a commissioner answerable to the government. Significantly, the Civic Guard was to be unarmed, but differed little from the RIC in structure, training or deployment. An estimated 97 per cent of the men recruited in the early months of the force were former IRA members and, of those, 30 per cent were veterans of frontline operations, including flying columns.[23] For the provisional government, time was of the essence as the membership of the RIC insisted, through its representative bodies, that before new police forces could be established in northern and southern

Ireland, their contract had to be honoured and completed, and the force had to be 'completely disbanded'.[24]

Despite the relative peace brought about by the Truce and the Treaty, tensions remained high as the RIC began to depart physically from its barracks. Old antipathies came to the fore, and some IRA Volunteers availed of a final opportunity to engage in violence against the police force they loathed. Gormanston Camp in County Meath was chosen as the depot where all members of the force would gather for disbandment. The Auxiliary Division was the first to be dispersed, with the last of its 1,243 members leaving Ireland on 25 January 1922. The Black and Tans, a group made up of members of the regular RIC recruited in England after 1919, was next, followed by policemen who had been serving in the force before 1919. On 3 March 1922, as the last police convoy left Tipperary town for Gormanston Camp, IRA Volunteers who opposed the Treaty placed a roadblock and called the convoy to halt. During the exchange of fire that followed, Head Constable Christopher Davis and Constable William Cummings were killed and several others were wounded.[25] The remaining policemen were taken prisoner but later released. Their vehicles, arms and ammunition were seized. The British government was subsequently informed that three of the surviving policemen had been arrested by the military as there were 'strong reasons for suspecting that this outrage was organised with the treacherous connivance of some members of the police party'.[26]

The chaos of the period just prior to the outbreak of the Civil War was encapsulated by Kevin O'Higgins, Minister for Economic Affairs in the provisional government. He wrote that the government was 'simply eight young men in the city hall standing amidst the ruins of one administration ...

with the foundations of another not yet laid, and with wild men screaming through the keyhole. No police force was functioning ... no system of justice operating; the wheels of administration hung idle, barred out of recognition by the clash of rival jurisdictions.'[27] The deteriorating situation and the imminent threat of Civil War made it imperative that new police forces were quickly established and deployed in northern and southern Ireland. In the transitional period leading up to full disbandment of the RIC, concern was expressed by the British government about the potential for discontented policemen to offer confidential information or equipment in exchange for money or guarantees of safety. It was of the utmost importance, therefore, to minimise any delay in disbandment. Mark Sturgis, Assistant Under-Secretary at Dublin Castle, cautioned the government that it could be a 'costly business if the value of the material surrendered is measured against whatever savings may be affected on the disbandment terms'.[28]

An audacious raid took place at Clonmel Barracks on 26 March 1922, during which the IRA seized three Lewis guns, 293 rifles and bayonets, 45 shotguns, 230 revolvers, 206,500 rounds of ammunition, 11 cars and a large quantity of other military equipment. A dubious Greenwood reported to the cabinet his belief that the raid could not have been carried out without 'culpable negligence, if not connivance, on the part of some members of the garrison'.[29] He also warned of the difficulty such incidents would cause to the new Irish administration. This concern was mirrored by Churchill, who was asked during a parliamentary debate if the provisional government was in a position to do anything about the disturbed situation in Tipperary. Referring to weaponry and personnel that had been supplied to Collins, including former

Black and Tans, Churchill informed Parliament that he was 'supplying the provisional government with the means of asserting their authority and that is their intention'.[30] General Sir Nevil Macready, Commander-in-Chief of British forces in Ireland, shared this concern and had written to the cabinet in March 1922 criticising the delay in disbandment. He stated that many policemen were now housed in military barracks for their own safety and, aside from the fact that they were still drawing pay, because they had nothing to do, they spent their time 'discussing their grievances, which if it continued might lead to trouble, with troops having to restore order'.[31] Writing to the chief of police in March 1922, Assistant Under-Secretary A. W. Cope highlighted the exceptional conditions in Ireland and noted that many members of the force would be in great danger if they remained at home after disbandment.[32] Chief Secretary Sir Hamar Greenwood concurred, stating that the bitterness of feeling in Ireland and 'almost impossibility of finding employment' placed the police 'in a radically worse position than any other public servants whose services have been dispensed with'.[33]

The British government did not accept the claims of RIC representative bodies pressing for better terms of disbandment that members of the force would be unable to live in any part of Ireland, but nonetheless the government did agree to a special payment for Irish policemen who wanted to move to England after disbandment.[34] In consequence of this decision, free railway warrants were issued, allowing policemen and their families to travel to any destination in Ireland or England.[35] Agreement was also reached that pensions would be adjusted to provide a living wage during what was termed the 'unemployable period' of several years that Irish ex-policemen were expected to face.[36] The British government estimated that about 8,000 men would be affected, with perhaps 5,600 of those expected to seek assistance with emigration or relocation.

The irony was not lost on police that facilities such as Gormanston Camp or Baldonnel Aerodrome, where they were now awaiting disbandment with their wives and children, had previously been used to detain Sinn Féin prisoners, and they became increasingly restless and militant.[37] On 14 March 1922 it was reported that several hundred policemen of all ranks awaiting disbandment marched from Ship Street Barracks to the RIC Depot in the Phoenix Park, and then on to Dublin Castle. Described by the press as 'hundreds of angry RIC men', their representatives issued a threat to officials that they would refuse to be disbanded 'unless increased compensation was forthcoming'.[38] This demonstration by a body renowned for rigid discipline echoed that of a previous generation of policemen when, in 1882, the strain of performing agrarian-related duties during the Land War led to several hundred RIC members unprecedentedly engaged in a brief public protest for improved pay and conditions.[39] During protracted negotiations with representative bodies and their legal advisors, Greenwood emphasised that the terms were the most generous ever granted by a government to public servants disbanded at their own request, but he conceded that such terms were fully justified, given the unique service rendered by the RIC.[40] Prime Minister Lloyd George agreed, stating that the loyalty and gallantry shown by these men had been such that 'it would be a dishonour for any government or party to neglect their interests'.[41]

On 27 March 1922 a circular was sent to RIC barracks informing all members that the disbandment of the force was to commence immediately, except in the six counties of northern Ireland, and that it was to be completed not later than 31 May. The RIC held its final parade on 4 April in the Phoenix Park Depot, which had been built as a training depot in 1842 and was the spiritual home of the constabulary. At the conclusion of this parade, the RIC effectively ceased to exist. Editorialising about the event, *The Irish Times* opined that a force that had given 'magnificent service to the Empire was not only being disbanded, but [was] being sent virtually into exile'.[42] Policemen based in Northern Ireland were allowed to remain serving until 1 June to allow transition arrangements to be made for the formation of the new Royal Ulster Constabulary (RUC). Recruitment advertisements for the new force specified that enrolment would be open to all members of the RIC, the Ulster Special Constabulary and a limited number of Dublin Metropolitan Policemen. It was also made clear that former members of the Black and Tans and Auxiliary Division would not be welcome; applicants with less than two years' service would only be considered in exceptional cases.[43] A total of 1,347 RIC veterans gained employment within the RUC, of which 505, or 19.2 per cent, were Roman Catholic.

Policing in Northern Ireland would prove to be as problematic and divisive as it had been in the south. The target of having one third of the RUC made up of Roman Catholics would never be achieved, as northern Unionists had been openly hostile towards Roman Catholic RIC members in many parts of the province. In September 1920, the British government permitted the formation of a special constabulary in Northern Ireland to bolster the RIC rather than deploy Black and Tans or Auxiliaries within the province. The Ulster

Special Constabulary (USC) eventually consisted of over 24,000 men in three cohorts: 'A' Specials – armed full-time policemen; 'B' Specials – armed part-time policemen; and 'C' Specials – unarmed part-time reserve policemen. Comprised almost entirely of Protestants, the USC was a controversial and divisive body, and came to symbolise the fractious nature of society in Northern Ireland after 1922. Many of its members were also members of the paramilitary Ulster Volunteer Force (UVF).[44]

Greenwood told Parliament on 5 April 1922 that, in accordance with the unanimous wish of the officers and men of the RIC, the government had decided to disband the force completely. Policemen were informed that, in addition to compensation and disturbance allowances payable to them on disbandment, their fares and those of their families and dependents to any part of the United Kingdom would be paid by the government.[45] Disbanded policemen who expressed a willingness to emigrate were allowed to commute their RIC pensions into lump sums, which could be used to establish businesses or purchase property in their new country of residence. Between 1922 and 1924, 5,400 applications for commutation were made, with 3,600 of those applications approved.[46] A resettlement branch was established at Chester under the direction of Sir Ormonde de L'Épée Winter, former director of intelligence at Dublin Castle, and many policemen travelled to England with their families in search of a new life.[47] In 1962 former RIC Constable Thomas Shirley recalled that in the period after disbandment he met numerous former policemen in London, at 'Piccadilly, the Strand and Hyde Park', waiting to emigrate to other countries, or perhaps hoping to return to Ireland if and when it was safe to do so.[48]

Several countries, including Canada, Australia, New Zealand and South Africa, were contacted by the British government enquiring as to whether they required experienced constables or soldiers in their colonial police forces or military, but the response was overwhelmingly negative. The London Metropolitan Police had some vacancies, but while the commissioner expressed sympathy, he informed the Home Office that his force could not 'be made a place of refuge for RIC men'.[49] The chief reason given for rejecting such requests was a moratorium on police recruitment caused by economic hardship following the Great War. Another significant reason was that many of those countries already had substantial populations of Irish immigrants. Consequently, the negative reputation acquired by the RIC during the previous three years weighed heavily against any consideration of employing its former members. In March 1922, for example, the police commissioner of south Australia warned the governor general of the state that 'grave trouble' would be caused if former RIC men were recruited to his force.[50]

Even if disbanded policemen could join a police force elsewhere, there were profound financial implications in doing so, as their pension and gratuity entitlements would be severely curtailed and withheld for the duration of their service in a new police force. Questioning Greenwood in the House of Commons during a debate on the disbandment of the RIC, Sir John Butcher, 1st Baron Danesfort, a conservative member of parliament for York, commented that disbanded policemen could go into private employment or do anything in the world for which they had no training, but if they did the one thing for which they were trained they would 'suffer in their pockets'.[51]

Many former Black and Tans and Auxiliaries joined the Palestine Police, which was undergoing rapid expansion to allow for the withdrawal of British troops from the country. Of the 483 former RIC members who joined the Palestine Police, 229 were Irish, with the remaining 254 giving their place of birth as England. Their commanding officer was Hugh Tudor, who had performed a similar role as chief of police in Ireland in 1920. The deployment of this new force led to similar allegations of brutality and lawlessness as had been made in Ireland. In a letter to the commander of military forces in Palestine, Sir Henry Wilson, Chief of the Imperial General Staff, scathingly referred to the tactics previously used in Ireland, which were now being applied in Palestine. He acerbically wrote that Winston Churchill intended to govern the country with 'hot air, aeroplanes [and] Jews stiffened by 700 Black and Tans ... no doubt we shall have profound peace!'[52]

Despite the Truce, the Treaty and impending disbandment, danger was ever present for policemen throughout Ireland. In Tipperary on 8 April 1922, Sergeant Edward McConnell, who had been stationed at Castlefogarty and was awaiting disbandment, attended a dance at Richmond Barracks in Templemore. When he failed to return to the RIC barracks in the town, his colleagues initiated a search. His body was found in woodland at the Old Demesne in the town. He had been shot six times. A former soldier from County Tyrone who was engaged to be married, McConnell had served in the RIC for less than twelve months. In common with many other policemen, soldiers and civilians during this turbulent period, the circumstances of his death were never clarified, nor responsibility for it taken by any group. Policemen who had already been disbanded were also in constant danger. At 10.30 p.m. on 23 May 1922, three men called to a house near Newport in County Tipperary, where recently disbanded RIC Sergeant John Walshe was visiting his wife and three children. The men spoke to Mrs Walshe and asked to see her husband, stating that he was required at the local police barracks. When Walshe came to the front door he was shot several times and died instantly. On the same night, former soldier Patrick Galligan was also shot dead in Newport. It was reported that no members of the public attended the removals of either Walshe or Galligan, and that no inquest could be held, as jurors refused to attend.[53] In the aftermath of these killings, a campaign of anonymous posters and letters directed all former RIC members living in the area to leave Newport. Several disbanded policemen who lived in the town hurriedly departed.[54] Walshe, who had previously been stationed at Newport and Cloughjordan, was the last RIC member to be killed in Tipperary, bringing the total number of men killed in the county since 1919 to forty-six.

On 17 August 1922, 380 members of the new Civic Guard led by Commissioner Michael Staines marched into Dublin Castle to formally take it over from the Royal Irish Constabulary. As the Civic Guard passed through the gates, it was watched by a large crowd, including disbanded members of the RIC, some of whom saluted as a gesture of respect to their successors. During the ceremony, the tricolour was raised over the castle, before the garrison of the Second Battalion of the King's Shropshire Light Infantry marched out of Dublin Castle for the last time. General Sir Nevil Macready, Commander-in-Chief of British forces in Ireland, observed the ceremony and acknowledged that the Civic Guard was 'a fine body of men ... and enlisted from the same class as the RIC, i.e. the sons of small farmers'.[55] At Gormanston Camp, only 400 disbanded members of the RIC remained, but by the end of the month, they too had departed. Former RIC Constable Thomas Shirley recalled in 1962: 'I locked the gates on the evening of 31 August 1922, handed the key to Commandant Brennan of the Free State army. I then took the train for the boat and landed in London at 6 a.m. the following morning'.[56] With that symbolic gesture, the Royal Irish Constabulary ceased to exist after 108 years of service. Describing the passing of the RIC into history, Sir Hamar Greenwood stated in the House of Commons that disbandment had been an inevitable consequence of the Treaty – 'as an imperial force they were born, and as an imperial force they wished to die'.[57]

Conclusion

'How is it that the great political parties are shaken to their foundations and shattered in almost every generation by contact with Irish affairs ... whence does this mysterious power of Ireland come?'

Winston Churchill[1]

As the decade of centenaries of events between 1913 and 1923 takes place, there is inevitably renewed and substantial interest in the events that led to Irish independence. The need exists to give a detached and balanced view of the significant events and institutions of this period. The Royal Irish Constabulary must be considered not least among these, because of its role as a civic, peacekeeping force at a time of escalating violence and because of the breakdown of trust in its capacity to keep the peace. It is the duty of historians to examine this period, notwithstanding the extent to which their work might be used to support the arguments and assertions of partisan political figures and commentators. The historian Michael Hopkinson has written that, throughout Ireland, ambushes that resulted in the deaths of policemen or soldiers have left lasting impressions on the public consciousness and 'remain the stuff of legend'.[2] In counties that were particularly

(opposite) RIC constables at the RIC Depot, Phoenix Park, 1920. They are believed to be Black and Tans as they're carrying their revolvers in military 'cross draw' style, and their medal ribbons indicate extensive military service. *(Courtesy of the Garda Photographic Section).*

violent, tourists and locals alike are encouraged to visit the sites of IRA ambushes. While the heroic figures of the IRA are well remembered, those who died at their hands are less so.

In pure military terms, the substantial majority of attacks planned by the IRA failed, but nationalist historiography has in many cases romanticised the brutal and complex truth of a violent confrontation that, in some respects, was analogous to a civil war. This has ensured that the comparatively few military successes of the militant nationalist movement remain in the public consciousness. The Canadian historian Peter Hart observed that some of the policemen killed acquired a posthumous notoriety that arose from 'Michael Collins having ordered their deaths', but he also emphasised the importance of examining the lives of less well known, and some forgotten, victims of the conflict.[3] The reality of hostilities frequently differed from the romanticised and self-serving versions of events presented by militant nationalists such as Dan Breen and Tom Barry in their memoirs. The tone of nationalist accounts of the RIC was set in 1926, some four years after the force had been disbanded, when Piaras Béaslaí contended that members of the force were never policemen in the sense in which the word was then understood in free countries, and that their primary and essential purpose was to 'hold the country in subjection to England'.[4] Much of the subsequent historiography of the period from 1913 to 1922 concurred with his assertion, and the almost 500 members of the RIC killed during the period have generally remained as statistics or footnotes, anonymous casualties of a bitter conflict. Dispassionate statistics cannot give an accurate portrayal of the devastation wrought on individual policemen and their families.

One of the objectives of this book is to consider the perception in nationalist historiography of the RIC as a militaristic, colonial police force. This perception finds its origins in the circumstances under which the force was conceived, when disaffection in some rural districts led to outbursts of agrarian violence and efforts by the authorities to deal with them.[5] The Peace Preservation Force (PPF), a rudimentary police service established by Sir Robert Peel, which was first deployed in 1814 in the Tipperary barony of Middlethird, evolved into the County Constabulary in 1822 and became the Royal Irish Constabulary in 1867. The policing of agrarian violence necessitated rural policemen in Ireland to be armed and militaristic in character. With the passage of time, however, the RIC grew and evolved into a civil police force, generally focusing on routine law enforcement. This may have brought acceptance, as the people and police operated in a society in which disturbance became increasingly less evident. Policemen spent long periods in the same district, gaining not only valuable local knowledge, but also a measure of acceptance by the community from which the force was recruited. Policemen forged relationships and most found their wives among the local population. They worshipped in nearby churches, sent their children to national schools in the area and traded with local merchants and suppliers. Even Béaslaí would later acknowledge that a large number of the RIC, notwithstanding their training, had 'no hostility to their fellow countrymen, and shrunk from a conflict with them'.[6]

There is evidence, therefore, that the police force became hibernicised, and statistics have shown how policemen were overwhelmingly Irish by birth and Roman Catholic by upbringing. The sons of farmers, labourers and shop assistants, they joined the force because it was regarded as a good job with reasonable pay, prospects of advancement and a pension upon retirement. By 1913, 86 per cent of the force was Roman Catholic, and 98 per cent had been born in Ireland.[7] Kevin O'Higgins, a minister in the Irish provisional government, spoke realistically when he remarked of those aspiring to a career in the RIC that it 'was the height of ambition for most young fellows who happened to be five foot nine or thereabouts'.[8] Policing was perceived as providing stable employment over the long term. In 1919, for example, there were over 400 men out of approximately 9,000 in the force who had joined over thirty years before. Thus, it may be reasonable to suggest that when conflict erupted in 1919 policemen might have reflected the political views and the cultural assumptions of many of their compatriots. The sum of their party allegiances may never be precisely known, but it is safe to assume that they ranged from loyalist and unionist to parliamentary and advanced nationalist.

In the period from 1919 to 1922, geopolitical considerations may not have been a concern to many policemen, as they faced not only the routine of their daily duties, but also the possibility of displacement, injury or even death. The escalation of political violence fundamentally changed the nature of policing in Ireland and estranged the police from many of those whom they sought to serve. The gradual distancing of the police from their local communities in the period after 1916 provided the militant nationalist movement with what it perceived to be 'legitimate' targets.[9] Following the Soloheadbeg ambush and the subsequent campaign of attacks on barracks, physical separation intensified as policemen were forced to abandon small barracks in isolated rural areas and retreat to larger urban barracks that were easier to defend. Hundreds of barracks were destroyed or damaged in the period between 1919 and 1922.

RIC barracks destroyed or damaged, 1919–22

Vacated barracks destroyed	552
Vacated barracks damaged	121
Occupied barracks destroyed	25
Occupied barracks damaged	267

Source: RIC Inspector General's Monthly Reports, 1919–22. National Archives of Ireland, CO 904 series.

Statistical evidence shows that the majority of barracks were destroyed after they had been abandoned, and also that IRA attacks on occupied barracks, which were heavily fortified, seldom resulted in their destruction. The lack of success in destroying occupied RIC barracks was a key factor in causing the IRA to switch tactics from carrying out large-scale attacks on fortified barracks to ambushes by mobile columns under the leadership of officers appointed by GHQ. As violence escalated during 1920, the inspector general of the RIC pleaded with the government to send the military to assist his beleaguered force. Reinforcements arrived in the form of the Black and Tans and Auxiliary Division. The decision to engage in what has been categorised as 'non-Irish recruitment' had profound and lasting consequences. It effectively nullified the organisation as a civil police force, destroying the RIC without the necessity of the IRA militarily defeating it.[10]

Violence against the force between the outbreak of hostilities in January 1919 and its disbandment in 1922 resulted in a national death toll of 493 policemen. Of these deaths, 242, or 59.75 per cent, occurred in Munster. The level of violence in the province was even higher than that percentage suggests; in 1911, Munster's inhabitants accounted for just 23 per cent of the national population. Violence in the six counties of Munster during 1920 and 1921 contrasts with the relatively low level of documented violence in the region during 1919, when neither Waterford nor Kerry recorded any RIC deaths. It could be suggested that if war had indeed been declared against the RIC, it did not start in earnest until 1920. Such outbreaks of violence as did occur in 1919 may have reflected the actions of violent individuals who were prepared to act independently of national IRA or Sinn Féin policy. Thus, in Tipperary during 1919, two of the three fatalities occurred at Soloheadbeg, and may reflect the personal involvement of militants such as Dan Breen. Following the Truce of July 1921, the level of violence dropped sharply and such further RIC deaths as occurred were isolated incidents, reflecting lingering personal animosities rather than a definite IRA policy or strategic decision.

High levels of violence were evident in County Cork and, to a lesser extent, Kerry, Limerick and Tipperary. These were in contrast with the relatively low levels in County Waterford. The Soloheadbeg ambush skews the pattern somewhat. In that year, the four RIC deaths recorded in Tipperary were more than in any other Munster county, accounting for 40 per cent of the province's total. It is important, however, to consider any statistic relative to the overall size and population of the county. By that measure, too, Tipperary was the most violent county, having one RIC death per 38,000 inhabitants.[11] The next most violent county was Cork, with one RIC death per 39,000 inhabitants. In 1920, Cork was the most violent of any Munster county in absolute terms, with forty-nine RIC deaths – more than twice the twenty-four recorded that year in Tipperary. When these deaths are compared with the size of the respective populations, however, Tipperary is the more violent county, with one RIC death per 6,000 inhabitants, while in Cork there is one death for every 8,000 inhabitants.

In 1920 Waterford was the least violent county in Munster. Its three RIC deaths represented the lowest total of any county in absolute terms and, with one death per 28,000 inhabitants, it was also the least violent in proportionate terms. In 1921 Cork was the most violent county in absolute terms, with 40 deaths, followed by Kerry and Limerick. Tipperary and Clare ranked joint fourth. With one death per 11,000 inhabitants, Tipperary was proportionately less violent than Kerry (1:6,600), Cork (1:8,000), Clare (1:8,600) and Limerick (1:10,200). In 1922 Tipperary was more violent in absolute terms than any other county, with four RIC deaths. The second most violent, Cork and Clare, record two each, a position confirmed in relative terms. Overall, for the period 1919 to 1922, with forty-six deaths in total, Tipperary proved to be more violent in absolute terms than Waterford (8 deaths), Clare (30 deaths), Kerry and Limerick (38 deaths each), but much less violent than Cork (92 deaths). In relative terms, Tipperary emerged as the most violent county, however, having recorded one death for every 3,313 inhabitants. It was followed by Clare and Limerick, each with one death for every 3,474 inhabitants. Thus, Cork emerges as a relatively less violent county for the period as a whole, ranking fifth of the six Munster counties.

The disparate levels of violence in the counties are revealed even more clearly when RIC deaths are expressed in statistical terms, relative to a thousand inhabitants. The counties of Clare, Cork, Kerry, Limerick and Tipperary rank closely together in terms of violence towards the RIC. This suggests that, in statistical terms at least, it would be difficult to conclude that a policeman would be safer in any one county. What is clear is that he would be safest in Waterford; in two of the four years, the county did not record a single police death, and in the other two years fatalities remained in single figures. While there is not much to distinguish its violent neighbours to the west and south, the salient historical question might be why Waterford stands out against the rest of the counties in Munster. Much of this can be attributed to the presence of strong characters in the other counties, such as Breen and Treacy in Tipperary and Tom Barry in Cork. Some IRA commanders carried out activities in their counties on their own initiative, clashing with IRA headquarters in the process for not being amenable to military discipline. Some Munster counties also had a long tradition of rebellion and lawlessness, being categorised as 'disturbed' by the British Government in the early part of the nineteenth century. This legacy meant that some counties in the province had more barracks, police and military per capita than others. Consequently, when conflict broke out in 1919, the IRA had more opportunities for targets in the heavily militarised counties.

The pattern of violence against the police in Tipperary shows that incidents may be divided evenly into those in which a lone policeman was killed (eleven incidents), and those in which a number were killed (eleven incidents). The former incidents include assassinations of significant figures – those holding a critical leadership or strategic role, such as District Inspector Hunt in Thurles or Wilson in Templemore – and those singled out as being especially ruthless or assiduous in fulfilling their duties, such as District Inspector Biggs in Newport. The latter incidents were carefully planned operations involving the deployment of large numbers of Volunteers, and were relatively more likely to take place in the months leading up to the Truce in 1921. The introduction of flying columns greatly increased the professionalism and military efficacy of the Volunteers. In consequence, the number of policemen killed in individual ambushes, such as those which took place at Modreeny, Inches Cross or Kilcommon, increased exponentially. There are also many cases in which Volunteers exercised 'discretion' as to whether policemen captured during ambushes or while on patrol were interrogated and relieved of their weapons, or killed. District Inspector Potter, for example, was offered the opportunity to escape from captivity, but he declined. In other cases, such as that of Head Constable Igoe, Volunteers from Tipperary were sent to Dublin specifically to kill him. There are several possible reasons for such discrepancies, including the unwillingness of individual Volunteers to execute somebody in cold blood, or individual enmities between policemen and IRA members.

The geography and topography of Tipperary were significant factors in the history of militancy and rebellion in the county. Being adjacent to other active counties and primarily rural, with many mountainous areas, made it suitable for ambushes. Strong personalities within the militant nationalist movement were also important factors as to why Tipperary differed from its neighbouring counties.[12] The south Tipperary brigade became estranged from the Irish Republican Brotherhood because permission had been refused for an attack on a policeman in 1917, and subsequent events demonstrated that GHQ in Dublin only had tenuous control over the three Tipperary brigades. The Soloheadbeg ambush, for example, was carried out in contravention of orders issued by the IRA chief of staff. Breen told local Volunteers that the Lorrha ambush had been authorised by IRA headquarters, when in fact no such permission had been given. Séamus Robinson, officer commanding the Third Brigade when the Soloheadbeg ambush took place, would in later life strongly contest the version of events in the conflict given by Breen, pointing out that Breen had spent most of his time outside the county, took part in few engagements and never held officer rank in the IRA. Robinson also wrote a series of letters to both the *Irish Press* and *The Irish Times* on the subject, using the pseudonym 'Dalriada'.[13]

For a variety of reasons, some policemen took no active part in the conflict, while others actively assisted the IRA in a variety of ways, such as providing information about impending searches or arrests. Many Irish-born policemen were torn between doing their duty and their inherent sympathies towards the notion of Irish independence. Constable Eugene Bratton in Meath, for example, was sympathetic to the IRA and offered to resign from the force, citing his disapproval of the behaviour of Black and Tans in the county. The local IRA commander advised Bratton to remain in situ, however, because he 'was much more useful' as a serving member.[14] Other policemen, particularly those with long service, shrank from confrontation or conflict, in the words of Tipperary IRA commander Liam Hoolan, 'hoping to live long enough to draw their pensions'.[15] Referring to the long history of the RIC, one retired policeman wrote that the force 'had the military efficiency when we did not really want it. When we required it, it was not forthcoming'.[16] Describing the difficulties faced by members of the RIC in 1920, *The Times* editorialised that policemen whose training had been entirely that of a civilian police force were to a great extent 'unfitted for the present conditions, which are those of a singularly difficult war. All their tradition, grown into an instinct, makes them slow to use firearms.'[17]

The departure of the police and the military had significant economic consequences for towns and cities throughout Ireland. On 9 December 1921, *The Irish Times* predicted that the withdrawal of the military from the garrison towns of Ireland would be a source of profound regret and that 'towns which owed the greater part of their trade to the military would now be hard hit unless some compensating factor is supplied'. Hundreds of RIC barracks, courthouses and other symbols of British governance had been destroyed, and those that remained had been abandoned. On 25 February 1922, *The Nenagh Guardian* reported that the withdrawal of British troops from the Curragh Camp had led to serious unemployment in the town of Kildare and the surrounding area, with over 400 men losing their jobs in one week following the final departure of soldiers from local garrisons.

In common with other garrison towns, the people of Templemore had maintained close social and economic relationships with the occupants of Richmond Barracks for over one hundred years. Consequently, there were serious economic and social consequences when the army left for good. The war diary of the Northamptonshire Regiment, describing the handover of Richmond Barracks to the IRA on behalf of the Irish provisional government, acerbically referred to the IRA as a 'motley force calling itself the Irish army'.[18] When marching from the barracks to the train station, however, it was noted by the soldiers that 'the enthusiasm of the civil population, after their previous attitude towards British troops, was extraordinary'.[19]

For lengthy periods of its existence, the RIC was a conventional civil police force performing routine and frequently mundane duties. In the last two years, however, most of its members found themselves in an extraordinarily violent situation that was not of their own making. Seventy-eight per cent of the policemen killed in Tipperary during the conflict, or thirty-six out of forty-six, were Irishmen. When hostilities finally stopped, many IRA Volunteers accepted that the RIC had indeed been courageous opponents. This recognition was encapsulated in an incident that took place when Naas Barracks in County Kildare was formally handed over to local IRA commanders after the Truce. During the ceremony, an RIC officer queried if the IRA would retain the force as the new police service of the Irish Free State. A senior Volunteer commander remarked that if they had not dealt with the RIC, there would have been no Free State, stating, 'your fellows had the most local knowledge, which was too much for us. Anyhow, we want to have our police modelled on your old lot.'[20] Perhaps no greater compliment could be paid to the men of the 'old' RIC than the recognition by their former enemies that the disbanded force might have served as a suitable model for a police service in the newly independent Ireland.

On 28 October 1922, Garda Henry Phelan, accompanied by Gardaí Thomas Irwin and Thomas Flood, entered a shop in Mullinahone in south Tipperary to buy hurling equipment, as they intended to start a team in Callan, where they were stationed. It was hoped that such involvement in rebuilding communities after three years of conflict would help to integrate the new Civic Guard into society and establish it as the legitimate police force of the fledgling Irish Free State. A group of anti-Truce IRA Volunteers followed them into the shop and shot Phelan dead, believing that he was, in fact, his brother, a disbanded RIC constable.[21] Phelan was the first member of the Civic Guard to be killed. He died in south Tipperary, where the first police casualties of the 1919–21 conflict had also been inflicted. Policing in Tipperary remained fraught with danger – policemen continued to bear the brunt of the conflict, no matter what uniform they were wearing.

The year 1969 marked the fiftieth anniversary of the Soloheadbeg ambush, and on 21 January of that year a notice appeared in the births, marriages and deaths section of *The Irish Times* commemorating Constables James McDonnell and Patrick O'Connell, the two policemen killed at Soloheadbeg. It was published 'in proud memory of two fine Irishmen ... and their gallant Irish comrades of the old RIC'. As Elizabeth Malcolm observed, by that time the epithet 'old' had come into common usage to distinguish the pre-1919 RIC as a civil force from its final incarnation. The same term was also used to distinguish the IRA as a force legitimised by its role in the foundation of the state from an organisation that acted against the state. In the case of the RIC, however, the application of 'old' not only allowed a distinction to be made between Irish-born policemen and the British-born Black and Tans or Auxiliary Division, but it also allowed for a clear distinction to be made between two fundamentally different historical contexts. In the case of both the IRA and the RIC, the distinction between 'old' and 'new' implied tradition and honour, legitimacy and acceptance as opposed to dishonour.[22]

In May 2010, some forty years after the anniversary of the Soloheadbeg ambush, a new memorial garden was formally opened inside the grounds of Dublin Castle to commemorate over eighty members of the Garda Síochána killed in the line of duty since the foundation of the force in 1922. The garden also contains a plaque commemorating deceased members of both the Royal Irish Constabulary and the Dublin Metropolitan Police. The only memorials to the Royal Irish Constabulary that previously existed are located at Saint Paul's Cathedral and Westminster Abbey in London.[23] The installation of a memorial plaque at Dublin Castle, the former headquarters of the force, is significant. It can be argued that such gestures, combined with a willingness to look afresh at Irish history, are tacit acknowledgements that the 85,208 men who served in the RIC between 1814 and 1922, and the almost 500 who died in the 1919–22 period alone, are worthy of remembrance in equal measure to other victims of the conflict.

In March 2012, the government of Ireland announced the nomination of an expert committee of historians and academics to advise them on the development and delivery of a programme for the 'decade of commemoration from 2012 to 2022'. The Taoiseach stated that the committee would develop a comprehensive and inclusive programme of commemorations 'appropriate for the centenary anniversary of the defining period of modern Irish history ... in particular it will seek to set a tone that is inclusive and non-triumphalist, ensuring authenticity, proportionality and openness, while acknowledging the multiple identities and traditions which are part of the history of the island of Ireland'.[24] Historians who challenge the accepted historiographical version of events, or otherwise demur, have been categorised as revisionist, and their work deemed controversial. The American historian James McPherson, however, wrote that revisionism is the lifeblood of historical scholarship, and that history is a continuing dialogue between the present and the past. He went on to say that 'interpretations of the past are subject to change in response to new evidence, new questions asked of the evidence, new perspectives gained by the passage of time. There is no single, eternal, and immutable truth about past events and their meaning.' The RIC, along with the judiciary, the army and the civil service, were fundamental to the maintenance of British rule in Ireland for generations. The decade of commemoration presents an important opportunity for the role and legacy of each of these institutions to be reassessed and placed in context in the evolution of a new Ireland.

APPENDIX 1

RIC Barracks in North Tipperary, 1919

Thom's Directory of the United Kingdom of Great Britain and Ireland, 1919 (Dublin, 1919).

Nenagh District
Nenagh (HQ)
Beechwood
Dromineer
Killboy
Portroe
Puckawn
Toomevara

Newport District
Newport (HQ)
Birdhill
Clonalough
Kilcommon
Rearcross

Borrisokane District
Borrisokane (HQ)
Annagh
Ballinderry
Ballingarry
Carrigahorig
Lorrha

Templemore District
Templemore (HQ)
Borrisoleigh
Dovea
Goldings Cross
Loughmoe
Templederry
Templetouhy

Thurles District
Thurles (HQ)
Holycross
Littleton
Moyne
Newtown Hut
Roskeen
Shevry

APPENDIX 2

RIC Barracks in South Tipperary, 1919

Clonmel District
Clonmel (HQ)
Knockevan
Lisronagh
Newcastle
Kilmanaban
Kilsheelin

Killenaule District
Killenaule (HQ)
Ballingarry
Drangan
Earlshill
Kilcooly
The Commons

Carrick-on-Suir District
Carrick-on-Suir (HQ)
Carrickbeg
Cloneen
Glenbower
Mullinahone

Cashel District
Cashel (HQ)
Ballinure
Fethard
Golden
New Inn

Cappawhite District
Cappawhite (HQ)
Clonoulty Hut
Dundrum
Hollyford
Kilfeacle

Cahir District
Cahir (HQ)
Ardfinnan
Ballylooby
Ballyporeen
Clogheen
Rehill

Tipperary District
Tipperary (HQ)
Glenbane
Bansha
Limerick Junction
Emly
Lisvernane

APPENDIX 3

RIC Deaths in County Tipperary, 1919–22

Date	RIC No.	Rank	Surname	Forename	Location
21/1/1919	50616	Con.	McDonnell	James	Soloheadbeg
21/1/1919	61889	Con.	O Connell	Patrick	Soloheadbeg
23/6/1919	55727	DI	Hunt	Michael	Thurles
20/1/1920	65234	Con.	Finnegan	Luke	Thurles
4/3/1920	69188	Con.	Heanue	John Martin	Bouladuff
17/3/1920	69198	Con.	Healy	Charles	Toomevara
17/3/1920	67945	Con.	Rocke	James	Toomevara
9/4/1920	62909	Con.	Finn	William	Lackamore Wood
9/4/1920	67704	Con.	McCarthy	Daniel	Lackamore Wood
10/5/1920	55303	Sgt.	McDonnell	Patrick	Goold's Cross
25/6/1920	61494	Con.	Horan	Michael	Unknown
2/7/1920	57569	Sgt.	Tobin	Robert	Ballinure
12/7/1920	71609	Sgt.	Stokes	John	Rearcross
16/8/1920	50239	DI	Wilson	William	Templemore
2/9/1920	54833	Sgt.	Brady	Philip	Lorrha
29/9/1920	64194	Con.	Flood	Terence	Killoskehan
29/9/1920	70978	Con.	Noonan	Edward	Killoskehan
3/11/1920	71234	Con.	Maxwell	William	Cloughjordan
13/11/1920	74436	Con.	Bustrock	Charles	Inches Cross
13/11/1920	62820	Con.	Mackessy	Patrick	Inches Cross
13/11/1920	71096	Con.	Miller	John	Inches Cross
13/11/1920	65367	Con.	O'Leary	Jeremiah	Inches Cross

Date	RIC No.	Rank	Surname	Forename	Location
6/12/1920	70628	Con.	Halford	Patrick	Kilcommon
6/12/1920	73877	Con.	Harden	Ernest	Kilcommon
6/12/1920	72263	Con.	Palmer	Albert	Kilcommon
6/12/1920	73844	Con.	Smith	Arthur	Kilcommon
0/12/1920	58456	Sgt.	Walsh	Thomas	Glenbower
17/1/1921	70823	Con.	Boyd	Robert	Cappawhite
14/2/1921	62113	Con.	Carroll	John	Ballywilliam
4/3/1921	74691	Con.	Beasant	James	Cashel
20/3/1921	62454	Con.	Campbell	William	Mullinahone
27/4/1921	59414	DI	Potter	Gilbert	Clogheen
6/5/1921	57392	Sgt.	Kingston	James	Newtown
14/5/1921	76116	DI	Biggs	Harry	Coolboreen
15/5/1921	71087	Con.	Nutley	John	Bansha
2/6/1921	70463	Con.	Briggs	James	Modreeney
2/6/1921	52669	Con.	Cantlon	John	Modreeney
2/6/1921	65453	Con.	Feeney	Martin	Modreeney
2/6/1921	55430	Con.	Walsh	William	Modreeney
30/6/1921	71315	Con.	Bourke	Joseph	Templemore
1/7/1921	70853	Con.	Shelsher	Joseph	Bansha
3/3/1922	59253	HC	Davis	Christopher	Tipperary Town
3/3/1922	74240	Con.	Cummings	William	Tipperary Town
8/4/1922	71243	Sgt.	McConnell	Edward	Templemore
20/5/1922	58985	Sgt.	Walsh	John	Newport

Endnotes

Introduction: 'Omnipotent and Omniscient'

1 Louis Paul-Dubois, *Contemporary Ireland* (Dublin, 1908), p. 183. French author Paul-Dubois described the RIC as 'secret police ... omnipotent and omniscient'.

2 *Constabulary Gazette*, September 1916.

3 James Herlihy, *Royal Irish Constabulary Officers: A Biographical Dictionary and Genealogical Guide, 1816–1922* (Dublin, 2005), p. 24.

4 Liverpool to Peel, 28 January 1816 (Peel papers, B. M., Add. MS40181); quoted in Galen Broeker, *Rural Disorder and Police Reform in Ireland, 1812–36* (London, 1970), p. 1.

5 Norman Gash, *Mr Secretary Peel: The Life of Sir Robert Peel to 1830* (New York, 1971), also Douglas Hurd, *Sir Robert Peel: A Biography* (London, 2007).

6 Peel to Liverpool, 15 October 1813 (Liverpool papers, B. M., Add. MS38195); quoted in Broeker, *op. cit.*, p. 2.

7 Peel to Abbot, 25 December 1816 (Peel papers, i, 236), quoted in Broeker, *op. cit.,* p. 25.

8 Whitworth to Peel, 18 November 1813 (Peel papers, B. M., Add. MS40187), quoted in Broeker, *op. cit.*, p. 6.

9 Con Costello, *A Most Delightful Station* (Dublin, 1996), p. 23.

10 *Ibid.*, p. 21.

11 Trevor May, *Military Barracks* (Buckinghamshire, 2002), p. 8.

12 Thomas Bartlett and Keith Jeffery, *A Military History of Ireland* (Cambridge, 1996), p. 358.

13 See Allan Blackstock, *An Ascendancy Army: The Irish Yeomanry, 1796–1834* (Dublin, 1998) and Ivan F. Nelson, *The Irish Militia, 1793–1802* (Dublin, 2007).

14 *An Act for improving the police of the City of Dublin, 1786*, 26 Geo. 3, c. 24.

15 S. J. Connolly, *The Oxford Companion to Irish History* (New York, 2011), p. 172.

16 Robert Curtis, *The History of the Royal Irish Constabulary* (London, 1869), quoted in Seamus Breathnach, *The Irish Police: From Earliest Times to the Present Day* (Dublin, 1974), p. 25.

17 Stanley H. Palmer, *Police and Protest in England and Ireland 1780–1850* (Cambridge, 1988), p. 205.
18 Norman Gash, *Peel* (New York, 1976) – a condensed version of *Mr Secretary Peel: The Life of Sir Robert Peel to 1830* (London, 1961) and *Sir Robert Peel: The Life and Times of Sir Robert Peel to 1830* (London, 1972) – p. 36.
19 Donal O'Sullivan, *The Irish Constabularies, 1822–1922: A Century of Policing in Ireland* (Kerry, 1999), p. 29.
20 Originating in Tipperary in 1806, by 1811 these groups were active in eleven counties, seeking to halt evictions, regulate rents and raise wages for labourers. Members of such societies were oath-bound to each other, and severe punishment was inflicted on those who broke the oath.
21 Wellesley to Peel, 1 May 1822 (PRO, HO 100/204), quoted in Broeker, *op. cit.*, p. 141.
22 Broeker, *op. cit.*
23 Palmer, *op. cit.*
24 George Cornewall Lewis, *On Local Disturbances in Ireland: And on the Irish Church Question* (London, 1836), p. 3.
25 Michael Hopkinson, *The Irish War of Independence* (Dublin, 2002), p. 4.
26 Louis Paul-Dubois, *Contemporary Ireland* (Dublin, 1908), p. 183.
27 Larcom to Edward Cardwell, 24 March 1860 (NLI Larcom Papers, MS7617/56), quoted in Lowe and Malcolm, 'The domestication of the Royal Irish Constabulary', *Irish Economic and Social History*, Vol. XIX 1992, p. 28.
28 Charles Townshend, *Political Violence in Ireland: Government and Resistance since 1848* (Oxford, 1983).
29 Lowe and Malcolm, *op. cit.*
30 *The Royal Irish Constabulary Manual; Or Guide to the Discharge of Police Duties* (6th edition, Dublin, 1909), p. 30.
31 David Fitzpatrick, *Politics and Irish Life 1913–1921: Provincial Experiences of War and Revolution* (Cork, 1998), p. 5.
32 Thomas Fennell, *The Royal Irish Constabulary* (Dublin, 2003), p. 175.
33 Robert Curtis, *A History of the Royal Irish Constabulary* (2nd edition, Dublin, 1871), p. 43.
34 Connolly, *op. cit.*, p. 633.
35 Robert Kee, *The Green Flag: A History of Irish Nationalism* (London, 1972), p. 270.
36 On Saint Patrick's Day 1858 a new revolutionary society, the Irish Republican Brotherhood (IRB) was launched by former Young Irelander James Stephens. The new secret movement was dedicated to the establishment of a democratic Irish Republic. The epithet 'Fenian', a reference to ancient Irish warriors, originated with a corresponding

branch of the organisation in America led by John O'Mahony and, by extension, eventually came to describe the movement in Ireland. See Noel Delahunty, 'The Aftermath of the Fenian Rising in County Tipperary', *Tipperary Historical Journal, 2009* and Bernadette Whelan, *American Government in Ireland, 1790–1913: A History of the US Consular Service* (Manchester, 2010).

37 Tom Garvin, *The Evolution of Irish National Politics* (Dublin, 1983), p. 61. For further information on militant nationalism in County Tipperary, see Gerard Moran, 'The Fenians and Tipperary Politics, 1868–1880', *Tipperary Historical Journal*, 1994; Clare Murphy, 'North Tipperary in the Year of the Fenian Rising, Parts 1 & 2', *Tipperary Historical Journal*, 1995–6; Brian Sayers, 'Attempted Rising – July 1848', *Tipperary Historical Journal*, 2005; Noel Delahunty, 'Fugitives and Flying Columns: The Aftermath of the Fenian Rising in County Tipperary', *Tipperary Historical Journal*, 2009.

38 F. S. L. Lyons, *Ireland since the Famine* (London, 1971), p. 28.

39 Robert Curtis, *The History of the Royal Irish Constabulary* (London, 1869), p. 191.

40 Stanley Palmer, *Police and Protest in England and Ireland 1780–1850* (Cambridge, 1988), p. 561.

41 G. M. Young and W. D. Handcock, *English Historical Documents, 1874–1914* V.10, (London, 1996), p. 84.

42 Boycotting was a powerful weapon in rural Ireland. In 1828, for example, during a speech at Clonmel Assizes, Richard Lalor Sheil, an associate of Daniel O'Connell, campaigner for Catholic emancipation and co-founder of the Catholic Association, referred to the practice: 'The government may withdraw their witnesses from the country and afford them protection; but their wives, their offspring, their parents, their brothers and sisters, nay, their remotest relatives cannot be secure, and the vengeance of the ferocious peasantry, if defrauded of its more immediate and natural object, will satiate itself with some other victim.' Thomas MacNevin, *The Speeches of Richard Lalor Sheil* (Dublin, 1845), p. 62.

43 *The Freeman's Journal*, 5 August 1882.

44 W. J. Lowe, 'The Constabulary Agitation of 1882', *Irish Historical Studies*, XXXI, No. 121 (May 1998), pp. 37–59.

45 Michael Hopkinson, *op. cit.*, p. 71.

46 W. J. Lowe and E. L. Malcolm, 'The Domestication of the Royal Irish Constabulary', *Irish Economic and Social History*, Vol. XIX 1992, p. 35.

47 Statement of Edmond O'Brien, BMH/WS.597, p. 15.

48 John D. Brewer, *The Royal Irish Constabulary: An Oral History* (Belfast, 1990), p. 9.

49 Brewer, *op. cit.*, p. 7.

50 Stanley Palmer, *Police and Protest in England and Ireland 1780–1850* (Cambridge, 1988), p. 555.
51 RIC Inspector General's Monthly Report, December 1918, NAI.CO 904/107.
52 Dorothy Macardle, *The Irish Republic: A Documented Chronicle of the Anglo-Irish Conflict and the Partitioning of Ireland, with a Detailed Account of the Period 1916–1923* (Dublin, 1951), p. 42.
53 P. S. O'Hegarty, *A History of Ireland under the Union, 1801–1922* (London, 1952), pp. 401–4. Other works by O'Hegarty include *The Victory of Sinn Féin* (Dublin, 1924). See *The Oxford Companion to Irish History* (New York, 2011), p. 427.
54 Statement of Eamon O'Duibhir, BMH/WS.1403, p. 25.
55 *Ibid.*
56 Dan Breen, *My Fight for Irish Freedom* (Dublin, 1924), p. 34.
57 Elizabeth Malcolm, *The Irish Policeman 1822–1922: A Life* (Dublin, 2006), p. 27.
58 M. L. R. Smith, *Fighting for Ireland? The Military Strategy of the Irish Republican Movement* (London, 1995), p. 7, quoted in Stephen Howe, *Ireland and Empire: Colonial Legacies in Irish History and Culture* (Oxford, 2000).
59 Stephen Ellis, *Tudor Ireland: Crown, Community and the Conflict of Cultures, 1470–1603* (London, 1985), p. 9, quoted in Howe, *op. cit.*, p. 7.
60 Joost Augusteijn (ed.), *The Memoirs of John M. Regan, a Catholic Officer in the RIC and RUC, 1909–48* (Dublin, 2007).
61 Thomas Fennell, *The Royal Irish Constabulary: A History and Personal Memoir* (Dublin, 2003). Fennell wrote an addendum just before his death in 1948, which strongly defended the integrity of the RIC from 1919–22, and was heavily critical of historians such as Dorothy Macardle and Piaras Béaslaí for the anti-RIC sentiments expressed in their works.
62 Stephen Ball, *A Policeman's Ireland: Recollections of Samuel Waters, RIC* (Cork, 1999).
63 Douglas V. Duff, *Sword for Hire: The Saga of a Modern Free-Companion* (London, 1934).
64 Brewer, *op. cit.*
65 Elizabeth Malcolm, *The Irish Policeman, 1822–1922* (Dublin, 2006).
66 See W. J. Lowe and E. L. Malcolm, 'The Domestication of the Royal Irish Constabulary', *Irish Economic and Social History*, Vol. XIX 1992.
67 Richard Abbott, *Police Casualties in Ireland* (Cork, 2000), p. 7.
68 Patrick Shea, *Voices and the Sound of Drums: An Irish Autobiography* (Belfast, 1981). Shea became one of only two Catholics to attain the highest position in the Northern Ireland Civil Service, that of permanent secretary.

69 Anonymous, *Tales of the RIC* (London, 1921).
70 Sir Nevil Macready, *Annals of an active life, Volumes I and II* (London, 1924).
71 See Frank P. Crozier, *Ireland for Ever* (London, 1932) and *The Men I killed* (London, 1937).
72 David M. Leeson, *The Black and Tans: British Police and Auxiliaries in the Irish War of Independence* (Oxford, 2011).
73 Richard Bennett, *The Black and Tans* (New York, 1959).
74 J. A. Gaughan, *The Memoirs of Constable Jeremiah Mee RIC* (Dublin, 1975).
75 David Neligan, *The Spy in the Castle* (London, 1968).
76 Dan Breen, *My Fight for Irish Freedom* (Dublin, 1924).
77 Desmond Ryan, *Séan Treacy and the 3rd Tipperary Brigade* (Tralee, 1945).
78 There are several series within this archive, including the HO 184/1-43 series, known as the RIC general register. The HO 184/50-51 series deals with the Black and Tans and temporary cadets of the Auxiliary Division.
79 A detailed list of those service numbers is contained in James Herlihy, *The Royal Irish Constabulary: A Complete Alphabetical List of Officers and Men 1816–1922* (Dublin, 1999).
80 These are arranged alphabetically on a county basis in the CO 904/175-176 series.
81 These records are located in series HO 340.
82 The CO 904/906 series.
83 This significant archive is contained within the CO 904 series.
84 Series HO 184, series CO 903 and series WO 35, respectively. The T 192 series contains information about the expenditure on the force for the period 1920–22.
85 Evi Ghotzardis, 'Revisionist Historians and the Modern Irish State: The Conflict between the Advisory Committee and the Bureau of Military History, 1947–66', in *Irish Historical Studies*, Vol. XXXV, 13 May 2006, pp. 99–116.
86 Kent Fedorowich, 'The Problems of Disbandment: The Royal Irish Constabulary and Imperial Migration 1919–29', *Irish Historical Studies*, Vol. XXX, no.117 (May, 1996), pp. 88–110.
87 *Random House Unabridged Dictionary* (New York, 2006).

1. 'Six Dead Policemen': The Soloheadbeg Ambush and its Consequences

1 Republican prisoner in Spike Island prison, 13 October 1921, quoted in David Fitzpatrick, *Politics and Irish Life, 1913–21: Provincial Experiences*

of War and Revolution (Cork, 1998), p. 3. A 'peeler' is a colloquial term for a police officer based on the name of Sir Robert Peel who founded the Peace Preservation Force in Ireland in 1814 and the London Metropolitan Police in 1829. Policemen in Ireland and England were subsequently nicknamed 'bobbies' or 'peelers'. The term is still in common use in the UK.

2 H. W. Nevinson, 'Sir Roger Casement and Sinn Féin' in *Atlantic*, 2 February 1916, quoted in Edgar Holt, *Protest in Arms: The Irish Troubles, 1916–23* (New York, 1960), p. 101.

3 *Tipperary Star*, 6 May 1916.

4 Statement of James Leahy, BMH/WS.1454, p. 4.

5 Desmond Ryan, *Séan Treacy and the Third Tipperary Brigade* (Tralee, 1945), p. 23.

6 Statement of Dan Breen, BMH/WS.1739, p. 19.

7 Joost Augusteijn, *The Experience of Ordinary Volunteers in the Irish War of Independence 1916–21* (London, 1996), p. 55.

8 Statement of Edward McGrath, BMH/WS.1522, p. 4.

9 Statement of Tadhg Crowe, BMH/WS.1658, p. 2.

10 Charles Townshend, *The British Military Campaign in Ireland 1919–21: The Development of Political and Military Policies* (Oxford, 1975), p. 7.

11 Seán Gaynor, 'With Tipperary No. 1 Brigade in North Tipperary 1917–21, Part 1' in *Tipperary Historical Journal* (1993), p. 32.

12 Michael Hopkinson, *The Irish War of Independence* (Dublin, 2002), p. 116.

13 Statement of Dan Breen, BMH/WS.1739, pp. 15, 18, 19, 20.

14 Ryan, *op. cit.*, p. 56.

15 Statement of James Leahy, BMH/WS.1454, p. 35.

16 Statement of Edward McGrath, BMH/WS.1522, pp. 7, 10.

17 C. S. Andrews, *Dublin Made Me* (Dublin, 2001), p. 119.

18 Townshend (1975), *op. cit.*, p. 1.

19 W. J. Lowe and E. L. Malcolm, 'The Domestication of the Royal Irish Constabulary', *Irish Economic and Social History* (Vol. XIX, 1992), p. 46.

20 P. Lyons to G. Orpen, 22 November 1931 (NLI Orpen Papers, Ms 17785), quoted in Lowe and Malcolm, *op. cit.*, p. 36.

21 Statement of Tadhg Crowe, BMH/WS.1658, p. 8.

22 Statement of Patrick O'Dwyer, BMH/WS.1432, p. 9.

23 Statement of Dan Breen, BMH/WS.1739, p. 21.

24 Statement of Patrick O'Dwyer, BMH/WS.1432, p. 9.

25 Statement of Dan Breen, BMH/WS.739, p. 23.

26 Statement of Phil Fitzgerald, BMH/WS.1262, p. 4, 16.

27 C. S. Andrews fought with the Dublin brigade during the 1919–21 conflict and served as adjutant to Liam Lynch, leader of the anti-Treaty forces

during the Civil War. See C. S. Andrews, *Dublin Made Me* (Dublin, 2001), p. 119.

28 *The Cork Examiner*, 21 January 1919, *Tipperary Star*, 23 January 1919, and Robert Kee, *The Green Flag: A History of Irish Nationalism* (London, 1972), p. 632.

29 RIC Inspector General's Monthly Report for Tipperary, January 1919. NAI.CO 904/108.

30 *Irish Independent*, 23 January 1919.

31 *Tipperary Star*, 23 January, 1919

32 *Irish Independent*, 23 January 1919.

33 Ryan, *op. cit.*, p. 73.

34 Statement of Jerome Davin, BMH/WS.1350, p. 5.

35 Statement of Eamon O'Duibhir, BMH/WS.1474, p. 43.

36 *Irish Independent*, 27 January 1919.

37 Note on the IRB and the south Tipperary brigade. University College Dublin, Mulcahy papers, P7b/181, quoted in Hopkinson, *op. cit.*, p. 117.

38 Statement of Dan Breen, BMH/WS.1739, p. 24.

39 Risteárd Mulcahy, *My Father, the General: Richard Mulcahy and the Military History of the Revolution* (Dublin, 2009) p. 52.

40 Robert Kee, *Ireland: A History* (London, 1980), p. 180.

41 Ryan, *op. cit.*, p. 87.

42 Statement of Séamus Robinson, BMH/WS.1721, p. 6. Robinson also wrote a series of letters to the *Irish Press* and *The Irish Times* on the subject using the alias 'Dalriada'.

43 Statement of Richard Dalton, BMH/WS.1116, p. 4.

44 Statement of Michael Fitzpatrick, BMH/WS.1433, p. 6.

45 *The Manchester Guardian*, 24 January 1919, quoted in Maurice Walsh, *The News from Ireland: Foreign Correspondents and the Irish Revolution* (London, 2008), p. 64.

46 *Daily News*, 24 January 1919, quoted in Walsh, *op. cit.*, p. 65.

47 Patrick Shea, *Voices and the Sounds of Drums: An Irish Autobiography* (Belfast, 1981), p. 27.

48 RIC Inspector General's Monthly Report, January 1919. NAI.CO 904/108.

49 *An t-Óglách*, 31 January 1919.

50 RIC Inspector General's Monthly Report, March 1919. NAI.CO 904/108.

51 Ryan, *op. cit.*, p. 53.

52 Tim Pat Coogan, *De Valera: Long Fellow, Long Shadow* (London, 1993), p. 133.

53 Fitzpatrick, *op. cit.*, p. 10, 11.

54 Shea, *op. cit.*, p. 27.

55 W. Allison Philips, *The Revolution in Ireland, 1906–23* (London, 1926), p. 167.
56 A biblical reference, which refers to the field purchased by Judas with the thirty pieces of silver he received for the betrayal of Christ.
57 Philips, *op. cit.* p. 167.
58 Denis Gwynn, *De Valera* (London, 1933), quoted in Kee (1972), *op. cit.*, p. 649.
59 RIC Inspector General's Monthly Report, March 1919. NAI.CO 904/108.
60 Philip Fogarty, *The Parish of Thurles: A Civil and Ecclesiastical History*, Vol. 66 (Tipperary, 1967), p. 5.
61 Statement of Dan Breen, BMH/WS.1352, p. 11.
62 RIC Inspector General's Monthly Report, May 1919. NAI.CO 904/109.
63 Statement of Michael Davern, BMH/WS.1348, p. 11.
64 Richard Abbott, *Police Casualties in Ireland* (Cork, 2000), p. 39.
65 RIC Inspector General's Monthly Report, May 1919. NAI.CO 904/109.
66 Statement of Séamus Babington, BMH/WS.1595, p. 22.
67 Francis Costello, *The Irish Revolution and its Aftermath, 1916–23: Years of Revolt* (Dublin, 2003), p. 39; Hopkinson, *op. cit.*, p. 25.
68 Seán Gaynor, 'With Tipperary No. 1 Brigade in North Tipperary 1917–21, Part 1', *Tipperary Historical Journal* (1993), p. 34.
69 James Herlihy, *Royal Irish Constabulary Officers: A Biographical Dictionary and Genealogical Guide, 1816–1922* (Dublin, 2005), p. 171.
70 Statement of Patrick Kinnane, BMH/WS.1475, p. 10.
71 Statement of James Leahy, BMH/WS.1454, p. 18.
72 Statement of Jerry Ryan, BMH/WS.1487, p. 5.
73 RIC special branch file on Ernest Blythe, NAI.CO 904/193/14A, p. 12.
74 *Irish Independent*, 25 June 1919.
75 Statement of James Leahy, BMH/WS.1454, p. 19.
76 *Irish Independent*, 25 June 1919.
77 RIC County Inspector's Monthly Report, June 1919. NAI.CO 904/109.
78 *Irish Independent*, 30 June 1919.
79 RIC Inspector General's Monthly Report, May 1919. NAI.CO 904/109.
80 RIC Inspector General's Monthly Report, June 1919. NAI.CO 904/109.
81 Townshend (1975), *op. cit.*, p. 27.
82 RIC Inspector General's Monthly Report, July 1919. NAI.CO 904/109.
83 Costello, *op. cit.*, p. 41.
84 Dan Breen, *My Fight for Irish Freedom* (Dublin, 1924), p. 54.
85 RIC Inspector General's Monthly Report, December 1919, NAI.CO 904/110.
86 RIC 'Outrages against the Police' reports, which commenced in April 1920. NAI.CO 904/148 series.

87 Statement of James Hewitt, BMH/WS.1465, p. 8.
88 RIC Inspector General's Monthly Report, August 1919. NAI.CO 904/109.
89 Statement of Martin Needham, BMH/WS.1323, pp. 5, 6, 8.
90 *Irish Independent*, 9 September 1919.
91 Statement of Martin Needham, BMH/WS.1323, p. 8.
92 RIC Inspector General's Monthly Report, September 1919. NAI.CO 904/110.
93 Statement of Séan Gaynor, BMH/WS.1389, p. 25.
94 RIC County Inspector's Monthly Report, September 1919. NAI.CO 904/110.
95 W. J. Lowe, 'Who Were the Black and Tans?' in *History Ireland* (autumn, 2004), p. 47; Cabinet conversation, 30 April 1920, CAB.23 20, quoted in Townshend (1975), *op. cit.*, p. 40.
96 RIC Inspector General's Monthly Report, October 1919, NAI.CO 904/110.
97 RIC Inspector General's Monthly Report, November 1919, NAI.CO 904/110.
98 Cabinet, 2 June 1921. Jones, Whitehall Diary, iii.73, quoted in Townshend (1975), *op. cit.*, p. 40.
99 Lloyd George to Bonar Law, 30 December 1919. Lloyd George papers, F/31/1/16, quoted in Townshend (1975), *op. cit.*, p. 45.
100 Hopkinson, *op. cit.*, p. 32.
101 Charles Townshend, *Political Violence in Ireland: Government and Resistance since 1848* (Oxford, 1983), p. 335.
102 Fitzpatrick, *op. cit.*, p. 15.
103 Peter Hart, *The IRA at War 1916–23* (Oxford, 2003), p. 74.
104 David Fitzpatrick (ed.), *British Intelligence Reports in Ireland, 1920–21: The Final Reports* (Cork, 2002), p. 64.
105 RIC Inspector General's Monthly Report, December 1919. NAI.CO 904/110.
106 Joost Augusteijn, *The Memoirs of John M. Regan, a Catholic Officer in the RIC and RUC, 1909–48* (Dublin, 2007), p. 116.
107 RIC Inspector General's Monthly Report, February 1920. NAI.CO 904/111.
108 Safety of Barracks: RIC circular D.94/1919. NAI.HO 184/125.
109 RIC Inspector General's Monthly Report, December 1919. NAI.CO 904/110.
110 Statement of James Leahy, BMH/WS.1454, p. 22.
111 Piaras Béaslaí, *Michael Collins and the Making of a New Ireland* (Dublin, 1926), p. 260.
112 GHQ Ireland, *Record*, ii.5, quoted in Townshend (1975), *op. cit.*, p. 42.
113 C.J.C. Street, *The Administration of Ireland, 1920* (London, 1921), p. 73.

114 Statement of James Leahy, BMH/WS.1454, pp. 22, 24.
115 RIC County Inspector's report, Tipperary North Riding. January 1920. NAI.CO 904/112.
116 Statement of James Leahy, BMH/WS.1454, p. 26.
117 *The Freeman's Journal*, 26 January 1920.
118 Much attention was focused on this story, as Finnegan received a blood transfusion, which was a relatively recent development in Ireland at that time. *The Irish Times,* 23 January 1920.
119 *Connacht Tribune*, 31 January 1920.
120 RIC Inspector General's Monthly Report, January 1920. NAI.CO 904/111.
121 Statement of James Leahy, BMH/WS.1454, p. 27.
122 *The Irish Times*, 22 January 1920.
123 RIC Inspector General's Monthly Report, January 1920. NAI.CO 904/111.
124 Hopkinson, Michael (ed.), *The Last Days of Dublin Castle: The Diaries of Mark Sturgis* (Dublin, 1999), p. 28.
125 Abbott, *op. cit.*, p. 51.
126 Charles Townshend, *Britain's Civil Wars: Counterinsurgency in the Twentieth Century* (London, 1986), p. 59.
127 Statement of James Leahy, BMH/WS.1454, p. 27.
128 Statement of Edward McGrath, BMH/WS.1522, p. 14.
129 Joost Augusteijn, *From Public Defiance to Guerrilla Warfare: The Experience of Ordinary Volunteers in the Irish War of Independence 1916–21* (Dublin, 1996), p. 270.
130 Statement of John Hackett, BMH/WS.1388, p. 6.
131 Statement of Seán Gaynor, BMH/WS.1389, p. 26.
132 Statement of John Hackett, BMH/WS.1388, p. 6.
133 Statement of Seán Gaynor, BMH/WS.1389, p. 26.
134 Statement of John Hackett, BMH/WS.1388, p. 8.
135 Abbott, *op. cit.*, p. 65.
136 *The Nenagh Guardian*, 20 March 1920.
137 *Connacht Tribune*, 20 March 1920.
138 *The Nenagh Guardian*, 20 March 1920.
139 Statement of John Hackett, BMH/WS.1388, p. 10.
140 W. J. Lowe, 'The War Against the RIC, 1919–21', in *Eire-Ireland: Journal of Irish Studies* (Fall–Winter, 2002), p. 9.
141 RIC Inspector General to Under-Secretary, 4 October 1919, quoted in Townshend (1975), *op. cit.*, p. 30.
142 Keith Jeffery, *The British Army and the Crisis of Empire, 1918–22* (Manchester, 1984), p. 80.
143 Townshend (1975), *op. cit.*, p. 345.

2. An 'Outbreak of Shinnerea': March to December 1920

1 *The Weekly Summary*, 7 January 1921.

2 Edgar Holt, *Protest in Arms: The Irish Troubles, 1916–23* (New York, 1960), p. 201.

3 *Tipperary Star*, 20 March 1920.

4 *An t-Óglách,* 1 May 1920.

5 *The Weekly Summary*, 27 August 1920.

6 Reference made in *The Weekly Summary* of 7 January 1921 to the arrest of Sinn Féin supporters in Scotland for the possession of arms and ammunition, and the increasing sympathy for the movement internationally.

7 See *The Nation* (London), 10 January 1920 and the *Daily Mail*, 3 April 1920, quoted in Dorothy Macardle, *The Irish Republic: A Documented Chronicle of the Anglo-Irish Conflict and the Partitioning of Ireland, with a Detailed Account of the Period 1916–1923* (Dublin, 1951), p. 340.

8 Macardle, *op. cit.*, p. 341.

9 Frank Crozier, *Impressions and Recollections* (London, 1930), p. 251.

10 Holt, *op. cit.*, p. 201. William O' Brien (1852–1928), Member of Parliament for Mallow, was proprietor of *Cork Free Press* and a renowned orator. He was a leading member of the 'All for Ireland League' that preached 'conference, conciliation and consent'. See Padraic O'Farrell, *Who's Who in the Irish War of Independence 1916–1921* (Dublin, 1980), p. 119.

11 Holt, *op. cit.*, pp. 201–2.

12 Patrick Shea, *Voices and the Sound of Drums: An Irish Autobiography* (Belfast, 1981), p. 45.

13 Richard Hawkins, 'Dublin Castle and the Royal Irish Constabulary', in T. Desmond Williams (ed.), *The Irish Struggle 1916–1926* (London, 1966), p. 180, quoted in Maurice Walsh, *The News from Ireland: Foreign Correspondents and the Irish Revolution* (London, 2008), p. 70.

14 Statement of Constable Thomas Byrne, 9 April 1920, 'Outrages Against the Police' reports, April 1920, NAI.CO 904/148.

15 *The Nenagh Guardian*, 15 May 1920.

16 Statement of Patrick Cash, BMH/WS.1372, p. 5.

17 'Outrages against the Police' reports, April 1920, NAI.CO 904/148.

18 *Irish Independent*, 11 May 1920.

19 *The Nenagh Guardian*, 15 May 1920.

20 *The Freeman's Journal*, 12 May 1920.

21 'Outrages against the Police' reports, April 1920. NAI.CO 904/148.

22 Statement of James Hewitt, BMH/WS.1465, p. 8.

23 Volunteer Circular General Order Six (1920), Terence MacSwiney 1920 files. Cork Archives PR4/1/(File 1).

24 Michael Hopkinson, *The Irish War of Independence* (Dublin, 2002), p. 26.

25 Court martial documents in the case of R. V. William Tynan, quoted in C. J. C. Street, *The Administration of Ireland, 1920* (London, 1921), p. 130.
26 Street, *op. cit.*, p. 276.
27 Joost Augusteijn (ed.), *The Memoirs of John M. Regan, A Catholic Officer in the RIC, 1909–1948* (Dublin, 2007), p. 116.
28 David Fitzpatrick, *Politics and Irish Life, 1913–1921: Provincial Experiences of War and Revolution* (Cork, 1977), p. 33.
29 The Interim Report of The American Commission on Conditions in Ireland contains oral and written evidence gathered from witnesses in Ireland during 1920–21. Evidence collected by the commission was presented to its parent body, the American Commission on Conditions in Ireland, and published under the title 'Evidence on Conditions in Ireland'. It was published 'without colour or comment' in order to allow the public to judge what events were taking place in Ireland, but it had an acknowledged nationalist bias due to the refusal of the authorities to cooperate with the commission. *Interim Report of the American Commission on Conditions in Ireland* (Washington, 1921).
30 Statement of Séan Walsh, BMH/WS.1363, p. 4.
31 Statement of Paul Mulcahy, BMH/WS.1363, p. 10.
32 *Irish Independent*, 5 July 1920.
33 RIC Inspector General's Monthly Report, July 1920, NAI.CO 904/112.
34 'Outrages against the Police' reports, July 1920, NAI.CO 904/148.
35 Hopkinson, *op. cit.*, p. 119.
36 CSI Weekly Surveys (1920), Cabinet Irish Situation Ctee. papers II (Memoranda), CAB.27 108, quoted in *The British Campaign in Ireland, 1919–1921: The Development of Political and Military Policies* (Oxford, 1975), p. 214.
37 RIC Inspector General's Monthly Reports, July and August 1920, NAI. CO 904/112.
38 Ernie O'Malley, *Raids and Rallies* (Dublin, 1982), p. 42. O'Malley (1897–1957) was born in Mayo and took part in the 1916 Rising while a medical student in Dublin. From 1918 onwards he worked as a full-time organiser for the IRA and commanded their second southern division. Strongly anti-Treaty, he was imprisoned in September 1921 and was one of the last prisoners to be released in 1924. His literary abilities set him apart him from other IRA veterans who wrote accounts of the period. *On Another Man's Wound*, his account of the Anglo-Irish War, was published in 1936; *The Singing Flame*, dealing with the Civil War, was published in 1978; and *Raids and Rallies* was published in 1982. See O'Farrell, *op. cit.*, p. 128.
39 Paddy Kinnane, 'My Part in the War of Independence, Part II', in *Tipperary Historical Journal* (1996), p. 101.
40 Statement of Patrick H. O'Dwyer, BMH/WS.1432, p. 22.

41 Desmond Ryan, *Séan Treacy and the 3rd Tipperary Brigade* (Tralee, 1945), p. 139.
42 Statement of Patrick Kinnane, BMH/WS.1475, p. 21.
43 RIC Inspector General's Monthly Report, July 1920, NAI.CO 904/112.
44 *Tipperary Star*, 21 August 1920.
45 Statement of James Leahy, BMH/WS.1454, p. 35.
46 *Tipperary Star*, 21 August 1920.
47 RIC County Inspector's report, Tipperary North Riding, January 1920, NAI.CO 904/112.
48 Hopkinson, *op. cit.*, p. 80.
49 Operational Diary of the Northamptonshire Regiment in Ireland, 1919–23.
50 *The Irish Times*, 20 August 1920.
51 *Northampton Daily Chronicle*, 21 August 1920.
52 *Tipperary Star*, 21 August 1920.
53 Kinnane, *op. cit.*, p. 103.
54 Statement of James Duggan, BMH/WS.1510, p. 15.
55 RIC Inspector General's Monthly Report, August 1920, NAI.CO 904/112.
56 *Tipperary Star*, 19 August 1920.
57 *The Irish Times*, 18 August 1920.
58 *Thom's Official Directory of the United Kingdom of Great Britain and Ireland, 1920* (Dublin 1920).
59 *The London Gazette*, 25 August 1917.
60 Statement of James Leahy, BMH/WS.1454, p. 38.
61 Hopkinson, *op. cit.*, p. 127.
62 RIC Inspector General's Monthly Report, August 1920, NAI.CO 904/109.
63 Russell Gurney, *History of the Northamptonshire Regiment, 1742–1934* (Aldershot, 1935), p. 340.
64 *Tipperary Star*, 20 August 1920.
65 *Limerick Leader*, 3 September 1920.
66 RIC County Inspector's report for Tipperary North Riding, August 1920. NAI.CO 904/112.
67 *Tipperary Star*, 20 August, 1920.
68 *Tipperary Star*, 4 September 1920.
69 RIC general register, NAI.HO 184.
70 *Limerick Leader*, 23 August 1920.
71 *Tipperary Star*, 4 September 1920.
72 *The Irish Times*, 23 August 1920.
73 Harbinson, Peter, *Pilgrimage in Ireland: The Monuments and the People* (London 1991), p. 229.
74 *Tipperary Star*, 4 September 1920.

75 *Limerick Leader*, 20 September 1920.
76 *Western Australia Record*, 27 November, 1920.
77 Statement of Edward McGrath, BMH/WS.1522, p. 14.
78 Statement of James Leahy, BMH/WS.1553, p. 43.
79 Statement of Edward McGrath, BMH/WS.1522, p. 15.
80 *Limerick Leader*, 3 September 1920.
81 Statement of James Leahy, BMH/WS.1454, pp. 42, 44.
82 Statement of Dan Breen, BMH/WS.1739, p. 36.
83 Peter Hart, *Mick: The Real Michael Collins* (London, 2005), p. 71.
84 Statement of Dan Breen, BMH/WS.1739, pp. 37, 112.
85 Statement of James Leahy, BMH/WS.1454, p. 44.
86 Patrick Murray, *Oracles of God: The Roman Catholic and Irish Politics, 1922–37* (Dublin, 2000) p. 7.
87 Abbott, *op. cit.*, p. 127.
88 Statement of James Leahy, BMH/WS.1454, p. 42.
89 *The Freeman's Journal*, 30 September, 1920.
90 Kenneth Griffith and Timothy O'Grady, *Curious Journey: An Oral History of Ireland's Unfinished Revolution* (Dublin, 1998) pp. 158–9.
91 *The Freeman's Journal*, 30 September, 1920.
92 RIC County Inspector's report for Tipperary North Riding, November 1920. NAI.CO 904/112.
93 Census of the Commonwealth of Australia, 30 June 1933. Australian National Archives, CAC Nq 319.4 AUS.
94 Correspondence between the author and the Walsh family, Sydney, Australia, 12 July 2012.
95 Correspondence between Provincial and General, 5 September 1953, Christian Brothers Archives Sydney, PLD5/09/1953.
96 Correspondence between the author and the Walsh family, Sydney, Australia, 21 November 2011.
97 *Northampton Mercury*, 5 November 1920.
98 *Tipperary Star*, 6 November 1920.
99 RIC County Inspector's report, Tipperary North Riding, August 1920, NAI.CO 904/112.
100 *The Times*, 20 September 1920.
101 RIC Inspector General's Monthly Report, October 1920, NAI.CO 904/110.
102 Francis Costello, *The Irish Revolution and its Aftermath, 1916–1923: Years of Revolt* (Dublin, 2003), p. 91.
103 Statement of William Meagher, BMH/WS.1391, p. 6.
104 Statement of Séan Gaynor, BMH/WS.1389, p. 32.
105 Statement of Patrick Cash, BMH/WS.1372, p. 8.
106 Gurney, *op. cit.*, p. 340.

107 Statement of Liam Hoolan, BMH/WS.1553, p. 9.
108 *The Irish Times*, 8 November 1920.
109 Statement of Con Spain, BMH/WS.1464, p. 8.
110 Statement of Edward McGrath, BMH/WS.1522, p. 27.
111 *The Irish Times*, 6 November 1920.
112 GHQ Ireland, *Record, ii.18*, quoted in Townshend, *op. cit.*, p. 40.
113 'Outrages against the Police' reports, April 1920, NAI.CO 904/148.
114 RIC Inspector General's Monthly Report, November 1920, NAI.CO 904/110.
115 Shea, *op. cit.*, p. 29.

3. The Storm before the Calm: January to July 1921

1 *An t-Óglách*, 15 March 1920.
2 Note on the IRB and the south Tipperary brigade. University College Dublin, Mulcahy papers, P7b/181, quoted in Michael Hopkinson, *The Irish War of Independence* (Dublin, 2002), p. 117.
3 D/Training, 'Function of A. S. Units: Training Memo No. 2, 23 April 1920'. Mulcahy papers, P7/A/II/17, quoted in Charles Townshend, *Political Violence in Ireland: Government and Resistance since 1848* (Oxford, 1983), p. 337.
4 Statement of James Kilmartin, BMH/WS.881, p. 4.
5 RIC County Inspector's report, Tipperary South Riding, November 1920, NAI.CO 904/113.
6 Statement of James Kilmartin, BMH/WS.881, p. 10.
7 Statement of Paul Merrigan, BMH/WS.1669, p. 8.
8 *Irish Independent*, 16 November 1920.
9 RIC Inspector General's Monthly Report, November 1920, NAI.CO 904/113.
10 Wilson papers, including the Wilson diary, 29 September 1920, Imperial War Museum. Sir Henry Wilson (1864–1922) from Edgeworthstown, County Longford, was a close associate of Lloyd George and an avowed Irish unionist – he was involved in the 'Curragh mutiny' of 1914. He rose through the ranks to become Chief of the Imperial General Staff (CIGS) until his retirement in February 1922, after which he became an MP and chief security adviser to the new Northern Ireland government. In June 1922 he was assassinated in London by two IRA members, who were later executed. See Padraic O' Farrell, *Who's Who in the Irish War of Independence 1916–21* (Dublin, 1980), p. 157.
11 Peter Hart, *The IRA at War 1916–23* (Oxford, 2003), p. 45.
12 *The Freeman's Journal*, 18 December 1920.

13 Statement of Edward O'Leary, BMH/WS.1459, p. 16.
14 Statement of Edward John Ryan, BMH/WS.1392, p. 13.
15 Statement of William Hanly, BMH/WS.1368, p. 12.
16 *The Freeman's Journal*, 18 December 1920.
17 RIC County Inspector's report, Tipperary South Riding, December 1920, NAI.CO 904/113.
18 Statement of Edward Glendon, BMH/WS.1127, p. 4.
19 *Irish Independent*, 23 December 1920.
20 *Connacht Tribune*, 25 December 1920.
21 *Irish Independent*, 22 December 1920.
22 W. Allison Philips, *The Revolution in Ireland 1906–1923* (London, 1926), p. 192.
23 *Weekly Irish Times*, 25 December 1920.
24 Statement of Edward McGrath, BMH/WS.1522, p. 27.
25 RIC County Inspector's report, Tipperary North Riding, December 1920, NAI.CO 904/112.
26 Captain Hubert Ronald Phipps, M.C (Military Cross), intelligence officer of the 1st Battalion of the Northamptonshire Regiment, Richmond Barracks Templemore.
27 Statement of Edward McGrath, BMH/WS.1522, p. 28.
28 RIC County Inspector's report, Tipperary North Riding, December 1920, NAI.CO 904/112.
29 RIC Inspector General's Monthly Report, January 1921, NAI.CO 904/114.
30 Statement of James Leahy, BMH/WS.1454, p. 60.
31 *The Nenagh Guardian*, 22 January 1921.
32 Statement of Martin Grace, BMH/WS.1463, p. 7.
33 *Irish Independent*, 16 February 1921.
34 RIC County Inspector's report, Tipperary North Riding, January 1921, NAI.CO 904/114.
35 *The Freeman's Journal*, 13 June 1922.
36 RIC County Inspector's report, Tipperary North Riding, February 1921, NAI.CO 904/114.
37 Statement of James Leahy, BMH/WS.1454, p. 68.
38 Statement of Patrick Keane, BMH/WS.1300, p. 5.
39 Statement of Timothy Tierney, BMH/WS.1227, p. 9.
40 Statement of Edmond Grogan, BMH/WS.1281, p. 10.
41 Statement of Patrick Keane, BMH/WS.1300, pp. 6, 9.
42 RIC Inspector General's Monthly Report, March 1921, NAI.CO 904/114.
43 RIC County Inspector's report, Tipperary South Riding, March 1921, NAI.CO 904/114.

44 *Irish Independent*, 22 March 1921.
45 Letter from Constable Harold Redvers Danton Browne, RIC Castlefogarty, 17 January 1921 (original MS in possession of Mr Chris Billham, Hong Kong).
46 Statement of Maurice McGrath, BMH/WS.1701, p. 34.
47 Statement of Paul Merrigan, BMH/WS.1669, p. 13.
48 This phenomenon has been categorised as 'terror-bonding' or 'traumatic bonding', but was defined in 1973 as 'Stockholm syndrome', whereby victims display compassion, and on occasion even loyalty, towards their captors.
49 Statement of Peter Tobin, BMH/WS.1223, p. 11.
50 Statement of James Kilmartin, BMH/WS.881, p. 15.
51 RIC Inspector General's Monthly Report, April 1921, NAI.CO 904/115.
52 Statement of James Kilmartin, BMH/WS.881, p. 16.
53 *The Nenagh Guardian*, 30 April 1921.
54 *Irish Independent*, 29 April 1921.
55 *The Nationalist*, 18 May 1921.
56 Statement of John Sharkey, BMH/WS.1100, p. 14.
57 Richard Abbott, *Police Casualties in Ireland* (Cork, 2000), p. 226.
58 Statement of Andrew Kennedy, BMH/WS.963, p. 22.
59 Statement of Michael Davern, BMH/WS.1348, p. 54.
60 'Outrages against the Police' reports, April 1921, NAI.CO 904/150.
61 *The Freeman's Journal*, 10 May 1921.
62 Statement of Seán Gaynor, BMH/WS.1389, p. 38.
63 Statement of Sean James Hewitt, BMH/WS.1465, p. 8.
64 *Irish Independent*, 19 May 1921.
65 Statement of Seán Gaynor, BMH/WS.1389, p. 42.
66 *The Times*, 12 January 1921.
67 *Irish Independent*, 19 May 1921.
68 *Irish Independent*, 17 May 1921.
69 Abbott, *op. cit.*, p. 241.
70 *Irish Independent*, 17 May 1921.
71 *Irish Independent*, 23 May 1921.
72 RIC County Inspector's report, Tipperary South Riding, May 1921, NAI.CO 904/115.
73 Labour Party report on the commission of inquiry into the present conditions in Ireland, NAI.CO 904/180, p. 7.
74 David M. Leeson, *The Black and Tans: British Police and Auxiliaries in the Irish War of Independence* (Oxford, 2011), p. 206.
75 Charles Townshend, *The British Military Campaign in Ireland 1919–21: The Development of Political and Military Policies* (Oxford, 1975), p. 168.
76 Statement of Seán Scott, BMH/WS.1486, p. 10.

77 John Rutter Carden (1811–1866) earned the nickname 'Woodcock' because 'those who shot at him always missed'. It was also said of him that 'having so many enemies is the reason for him not being shot, for everyone leaves it for the others to do, and so he escapes altogether; whereas if he had only a few, he would be shot at once'. See Arthur Carden, 'Templemore Houses And Castles: Drawings by Robert Smith' in *Tipperary Historical Journal* (2002), p. 113.
78 RIC County Inspector's report, Tipperary North Riding, June 1921, NAI.CO 904/115.
79 Statement of Seán Gaynor, BMH/WS.1389, p. 43.
80 Statement of Liam Hoolan, BMH/WS.1553, p. 16.
81 *Irish Independent*, 4 June 1921.
82 Statement of James Leahy, BMH/WS.1454, pp. 77, 78.
83 *The Nenagh Guardian*, 2 July 1921.
84 Abbott, *op. cit.*, p. 285.
85 *Irish Independent*, 1 July 1921.
86 *The Irish Times*, 18 August 1921.
87 Weekly Survey of the State of Ireland, November 1921, National Archives CAB/24/131.
88 'Outrages against the Police' reports, July 1921, NAI.CO 904/150.
89 *The Freeman's Journal*, 4 July 1921.
90 Abbott, *op. cit.*, p. 264.
91 'Outrages against the Police' reports, July 1921, NAI.CO 904/150.
92 *Irish Independent*, 8 July 1921.
93 Padraig O'Haicead, *Keep their Names Ever Green* (Nenagh, 2003), pp. 162–163.
94 'Outrages against the Police' reports, April 1920, NAI.CO 904/148.
95 Statement of James Leahy, BMH/WS.1454, pp. 42, 50.
96 Michael T. Foy, *Michael Collins's Intelligence War: The Struggle between the British and the IRA, 1919–1921* (Gloucester, 2006), p. 185.
97 RIC service file for Head Constable Eugene Igoe. TNA: PRO T164/25/20, quoted in Foy, *op. cit.*, p. 185.
98 Michael Hopkinson (ed.), *The Last Days of Dublin Castle: The Diaries of Mark Sturgis* (Dublin, 1999), p. 28.
99 Townshend, *op. cit.*, p. 197.
100 RIC County Inspector's report, Tipperary North Riding, July 1921, NAI. CO 904/116.
101 RIC Inspector General's Monthly Report, July 1921, NAI.CO 904/116.
102 Patrick Shea, *Voices and the Sound of Drums: An Irish Autobiography* (Belfast, 1981), p. 27.

4. The 'Unemployable Period': Truce, Treaty and Disbandment

1 Michael Collins, 'Clearing the road – an essay in practical politics', in William G. Fitzgerald (ed.), *The Voice of Ireland* (Dublin, 1923), p. 42, quoted in Ronan Fanning, *Independent Ireland* (Dublin, 1983), p. 1.

2 Arrangements Governing the Cessation of Active Operations in Ireland', 1921, Cmd.1534 xxxix 427, quoted in Charles Townshend, *The British Military Campaign in Ireland 1919–21: The Development of Political and Military Policies* (Oxford, 1975), p. 198.

3 Weekly Survey of the State of Ireland, November 1921, National Archives CAB/24/131.

4 Memo from RIC Deputy Inspector General Walsh to all county and district inspectors, 9 December 1921, NAI.CO 904/178.

5 RIC County Inspector's report, Tipperary North Riding, August 1921, NAI.CO 904/116.

6 Piaras Béaslaí, *Michael Collins and the Making of a New Ireland* (London, 1926), p. 244. See Padraic O'Farrell, *Who's Who in the Irish War of Independence 1916–1921* (Dublin, 1980), p. 14.

7 Townshend, *op. cit.*, p. 199.

8 C. J. C, Street, *Ireland in 1921* (London, 1922), p. 258.

9 Memo from Chief Secretary to the cabinet on the future of the RIC, 10 December 1921, National Archives, CAB/24/131.

10 Joost Augusteijn (ed.), *The Memoirs of John M. Regan, A Catholic Officer in the RIC and RUC, 1909–1948* (Dublin, 2007), p. 181.

11 *Irish Independent*, 16 March 1922.

12 Timothy Healy (1885–1931), a King's Counsel and Member of Parliament between 1880 and 1918, represented six different constituencies and four different political allegiances. See *Oxford Companion to Irish History* (New York, 2011), p. 237.

13 Kent Fedorowich, 'The Problems of Disbandment: The Royal Irish Constabulary and Imperial Migration, 1919–29', *Irish Historical Studies*, Vol. XXX, no.117 (May 1996), p. 92.

14 Circular from the Chief Secretary's Office to all RIC stations, 17 December, 1921, NAI.CO 904/178.

15 Cabinet meeting minutes, agenda item 5, 12 December 1921. National Archives CAB/23/27.

16 Memo from Colonial Secretary Winston Churchill to the cabinet on the transfer of powers to the Irish provisional government, 11 January 1922. National Archives CAB/24/132.

17 Cabinet meeting minutes, 15 March 1922. National Archives CAB/23/29.

18 Fearghal McGarry, *Eoin O'Duffy: A Self-Made Hero* (Oxford, 2005), p. 52.

19 Gregory Allen, *The Garda Síochána: Policing Independent Ireland, 1922–82* (Dublin, 1999), p. 10.

20 Elizabeth Malcolm, *The Irish Policeman, 1822–1922: A Life* (Dublin, 2006), p. 215.
21 On 31 July 1923 the Dáil approved an amendment submitted by Cathal O'Shannon of the Labour party that the name of the Civic Guard be changed to 'Garda Síochána na hÉireann', or 'Guardian of the Peace of Ireland'. See Liam McNiffe, *A History of the Garda Síochána* (Dublin, 1997), p. 31.
22 Cabinet meeting minutes, 15 March 1922. National Archives CAB/23/29.
23 Conor Brady, *Guardians of the Peace* (Dublin, 1974), pp. 43, 47.
24 Fedorowich, *op. cit.*, p. 92.
25 *The Freeman's Journal*, 4 March 1922.
26 Weekly Survey of the State of Ireland, week ended 10 March 1922, National Archives CAB/24/134.
27 Kevin O'Higgins, address to the Irish Society at Oxford University, 1924, cited in Terence De Vere White, *Kevin O'Higgins* (Dublin, 1966), p. 84.
28 Fedorowich, *op. cit.*, p. 95.
29 Weekly Survey of the State of Ireland, week ended 27 March 1922, National Archives CAB/24/134.
30 Parliamentary question from Sir William Davison to Winston Churchill, 26 July 1922, *Hansard's Parliamentary Debates, Fifth Series, House of Commons* (vol. 51 cc 876–9, London 1909–42).
31 Memo from CIC Ireland to the cabinet, 11 March 1922, National Archives CAB/24/134.
32 Alfred W. Cope was Assistant Under-Secretary for Ireland and was involved in peace negotiations with the IRA. See O' Farrell, *op. cit.*, p. 37.
33 Letter from Chief Secretary Greenwood to the Treasury 24 February 1922, National Archives CAB/24/134.
34 Irish Office memorandum on the disbandment of the RIC, 24 February 1922, National Archives CAB/24/134.
35 Memo from Cope to Tudor, 29 March 1922, NAI.CO 904/178.
36 Irish Office memorandum on the disbandment of the RIC, 24 February 1922, National Archives CAB/24/134.
37 Fedorowich, *op. cit.*, p. 96.
38 *Irish Independent*, 15 March 1922.
39 W. J. Lowe, 'The Constabulary Agitation of 1882', *Irish Historical Studies*, xxxi, no. 121 (May 1998), pp. 37–59.
40 Summary of proceedings at interviews of RIC Representative Bodies with the Chief Secretary, 6, 7 and 8 February 1922, National Archives CAB/24/134.
41 Cabinet meeting minutes, 15 March 1922. National Archives CAB/23/29.
42 *The Irish Times*, 13 April 1922.

43 Richard Doherty, *The Thin Green Line: A History of the Royal Ulster Constabulary GC* (Yorkshire, 2004), pp. 20, 21.
44 Michael Farrell, *Arming the Protestants: The Formation of the Ulster Special Constabulary and the Royal Ulster Constabulary, 1920–27* (London, 1983), pp. 30–54.
45 House of Commons debate, 5 April 1922, *Hansard's Parliamentary Debates, Fifth Series, House of Commons* (vol. 152 cc 2235–9, London 1909–42).
46 Malcolm, *op. cit.*, p. 221.
47 *The Irish Times*, 2 May 1922.
48 Letter from former Constable Thomas Shirley 1962, *Murroe Boher Parish Newsletter* (Limerick, 2009), p. 52.
49 Fedorowich, *op. cit.*, p. 97.
50 Fedorowich, *op. cit.*, p. 101.
51 House of Commons debate, 5 April 1922, *Hansard's Parliamentary Debates, Fifth Series, House of Commons* (vol. 157 cc 1301–3, London 1909–42).
52 Fedorowich, *op. cit*., pp. 98, 99.
53 *The Southern Star*, 27 May 1922.
54 *The Nenagh Guardian*, 27 May 1922.
55 Memo to cabinet on the situation in Ireland for the week ended 19 August 1922. National Archives CAB/24/136.
56 Letter from former Constable Thomas Shirley, *op. cit.,* (Limerick, 2009), p. 52.
57 *Irish Independent*, 11 May 1922.

Conclusion

1 Churchill writing about Ireland in 1921, quoted in Martin Gilbert, *Winston Churchill: World in Torment*, Vol. IV, 1916–1922 (London, 1975), p. 201.
2 Michael Hopkinson, *The Irish War of Independence* (Dublin, 2002), p. 74.
3 Richard Abbott, *Police Casualties in Ireland* (Cork, 2000), p. 9.
4 Piaras Béaslaí, *Michael Collins and the Making of a New Ireland* (London, 1926), Vol. 1, p. 319.
5 See Galen Broeker, *Rural Disorder and Police Reform in Ireland, 1812–36* (London, 1970); James S. Donnelly, *Captain Rock: The Irish Agrarian Rebellion of 1821–1824* (Cork, 2009); and idem, *The Great Irish Potato Famine* (London, 2001).
6 Thomas Fennell, *The Royal Irish Constabulary* (Dublin, 2003), p. 174.
7 David Fitzpatrick, *Politics and Irish Life, 1913–1921: Provincial Experiences of War and Revolution* (Cork, 1977), p. 24.
8 Patrick Shea, *Voices and the Sound of Drums: An Irish Autobiography* (Belfast, 1981), p. 29. Kevin O'Higgins was Sinn Féin TD for Laois/

Offaly, and played a prominent role in drafting the 1922 constitution. As Minister for Home Affairs, he was responsible for reinstituting law and order as well economic recovery in the new Free State. He was instrumental in creating the Garda Síochána as an unarmed police force to replace the RIC, and became Minister for Justice in 1924. O'Higgins was shot dead on 10 July 1927 by the IRA while walking to mass. See Padraic O'Farrell, *Who's Who in the Irish War of Independence 1916–1921* (Dublin, 1980), p. 126.

9 Joost Augusteijn, *From Public Defiance to Guerrilla Warfare: Experiences of Ordinary Volunteers in the Irish War of Independence* (Dublin, 1996), p. 344.

10 W. J. Lowe, 'The War Against the RIC, 1919–21', in *Eire-Ireland: Journal of Irish Studies* (Fall–Winter, 2002), p. 35.

11 As recorded in the last available census data of 1911 (rounded to the nearest thousand).

12 Hopkinson, *op. cit.*, p. 116.

13 Statement of Séamus Robinson, BMH/WS.1721, p. 6.

14 Statement of Eugene Bratton, BMH/WS.467, p. 12.

15 Statement of Liam Hoolan, BMH/WS.1553, p. 13.

16 P. Lyons to G. Orpen, 22 November 1931. (NLI Orpen Papers, Ms 17785), quoted in W. J. Lowe and E. L. Malcolm, 'The Domestication of the Royal Irish Constabulary', *Irish Economic and Social History*, Vol. XIX 1992, p. 31.

17 *The Times*, 20 August 1920.

18 Northamptonshire regimental diary, 1919–23.

19 Russell Gurney, *History of the Northamptonshire Regiment, 1742–1934* (Aldershot, 1935), p. 341.

20 V. H. Scott to J. R. W. Goulden, 21 February 1968. Trinity College Dublin, Goulden papers, MS 7382a/68, quoted in W. J. Lowe, 'The War Against the RIC, 1919–21', in *Eire-Ireland: Journal of Irish Studies* (Fall–Winter, 2002).

21 Gregory Allen, *The Garda Síochána: Policing Independent Ireland, 1922–82* (Dublin, 1999), p. 72.

22 Elizabeth Malcolm, *The Irish Policeman, 1822–1922: A Life* (Dublin, 2006), p. 245.

23 James Herlihy, *The Royal Irish Constabulary: A Short History and Genealogical Guide* (Dublin, 1997), p. 18.

24 Government press release on the decade of commemoration, 2012–22, (www.merrionstreet.ie/index.php/2012/03/national-commemorations-programme-decade-of-centenaries-2012-2022) (Accessed 6 March 2012).

Bibliography

National Archives of Ireland, Dublin

Census of Ireland, 1911

Monthly Reports of District and County Inspectors of the Royal Irish Constabulary, 1919–21

Weekly Survey of the State of Ireland, Public Records Office London, CAB/24/131–132 Series

National Library of Ireland, Dublin

Interim Report of the American Commission on Conditions in Ireland, 1921

Labour Party Report on the Commission of Inquiry into the Present Conditions in Ireland, 1921

Bureau of Military History

IRA WITNESS STATEMENTS

Reference	Name	Brigade	Rank
BMH/WS. 1595	Séamus Babington	3rd	Brigade Engineer
BMH/WS. 1352	Dan Breen	3rd	Quartermaster
BMH/WS. 1372	Patrick Cash	1st	Vice-Commandant
BMH/WS. 599	Edmond Crowe	3rd	Volunteer
BMH/WS. 1658	Tadhg Crowe	3rd	Quartermaster
BMH/WS. 1116	Richard Dalton	3rd	Flying Column
BMH/WS. 1348	Michael Davern	3rd	Republican Police
BMH/WS. 1350	Jerome Davin	1st	Commandant
BMH/WS. 1510	James Duggan	2nd	Captain

Reference	Name	Brigade	Rank
BMH/WS. 1356	Tadgh Dwyer	3rd	Commandant
BMH/WS. 1262	Phil Fitzgerald	3rd	Adjutant/IRB Centre
BMH/WS. 1433	Michael Fitzpatrick	3rd	Flying Column
BMH/WS. 1259	Sean Fitzpatrick	3rd	Adjutant
BMH/WS. 1389	Seán Gaynor	1st	Adjutant
BMH/WS. 1127	Edward Glendon	3rd	Adjutant
BMH/WS. 1463	Martin Grace	1st	Quartermaster
BMH/WS. 1281	Edmond Grogan	3rd	Vice-Commandant
BMH/WS. 1388	John Hackett	1st	Intelligence Officer
BMH/WS. 1368	William Hanly	1st	Adjutant
BMH/WS. 935	Seán Harling	1st (Dublin)	Commandant
BMH/WS. 1465	James Hewitt	1st	Quartermaster
BMH/WS. 1553	Liam Hoolan	1st	Commandant
BMH/WS. 1300	Patrick Keane	3rd	Flying Column
BMH/WS. 963	Andrew Kennedy	3rd	Flying Column
BMH/WS. 881	James Kilmartin	3rd	Volunteer
BMH/WS. 1475	Patrick Kinnane	2nd	Commandant
BMH/WS. 1454	James Leahy	2nd	Commandant
BMH/WS. 1522	Edward McGrath	2nd	Vice-Commandant
BMH/WS. 1701	Maurice McGrath	3rd	Adjutant
BMH/WS. 1541	Thomas Meagher	2nd	Quartermaster
BMH/WS. 1391	William Meagher	1st	Flying Column
BMH/WS. 1669	Paul Merrigan	3rd	Transport Officer
BMH/WS. 1363	Paul Mulcahy	3rd	Commandant
BMH/WS. 1323	Martin Needham	1st	Vice-Commandant
BMH/WS. 597	Edmond O'Brien	Limerick	IRB Centre
BMH/WS. 1403	Eamon O'Duibhir	2nd	IRB County Centre
BMH/WS. 1474	Eamon O'Duibhir	3rd	IRB County Centre

Reference	Name	Brigade	Rank
BMH/WS. 1432	Patrick O'Dwyer	3rd	Captain
BMH/WS. 1392	Edward Ryan	1st	Volunteer
BMH/WS. 1487	Jerry Ryan	2nd	Commandant
BMH/WS. 1486	Seán Scott	2nd	Commandant
BMH/WS. 1100	John Sharkey	3rd	Intelligence Officer
BMH/WS. 1464	Con Spain	1st	Commandant
BMH/WS. 1227	Timothy Tierney	3rd	Captain
BMH/WS. 1223	Peter Tobin	3rd	Flying Column

University College Dublin Archives
Con Moloney Papers
Ernie O'Malley Papers

Tipperary Studies, Thurles
Canon Philip Fogarty, *The Parish of Thurles: A Civil and Ecclesiastical History*, Vol. 66

National Archives, Kew, London
Cabinet Meeting Minutes, 1921–2
Disbandment Forms of Option, 1922
Dublin Castle Records
The Dublin Police Act – 'An Act for Improving the Police of the City of Dublin, 1786', 26 Geo. 3, c. 24.
RIC General Register, 1816–1922
RIC Weekly Outrage Reports, 1920–21

Central Library, Northampton
Operational Diary of the Northamptonshire Regiment in Ireland, 1919–22

Imperial War Museum, London
Field Marshal Sir Henry Wilson GCB DSO Papers

Garda Síochána Museum and Archives, Dublin Castle
The Royal Irish Constabulary Manual or Guide to the Discharge of Police Duties, 6th edition, 1909

Garda College Museum, Templemore

Letter of Former RIC Constable Thomas Shirley, 1962

Letter of RIC Constable H. R. D. Browne, Castlefogarty, 17 January 1921

Cork City Archives, Cork

Volunteer Circular, General Order 6, Terence MacSwiney 1920 files, PR4/1

Newspapers and Periodicals

The Clonmel Nationalist
Connacht Tribune
The Cork Examiner
Daily Mail
The Daily News
The Freeman's Journal
History Ireland
Irish Independent
The Irish Times
The London Gazette
The Manchester Guardian
The Nation
The Nenagh Guardian
Northampton Daily Chronicle
Northampton Mercury
An t-Óglách
The Southern Star
The Times
Tipperary Star
Weekly Irish Times
The Weekly Summary
Western Australia Record

Official Publications

Hansard House of Commons and House of Lords Parliamentary Debates

Documents on Irish Foreign Policy Volume 1, 1919–22, NAI: DE/2/304/1

Thom's Official Directory of the United Kingdom of Great Britain and Ireland (1919–22)

Books

Abbott, Richard, *Police Casualties in Ireland* (Cork, 2000)

Allen, Gregory, *The Garda Síochána: Policing Independent Ireland, 1922–82* (Dublin, 1999)

Anderson, David M. and Killingray, David (eds), *Policing and Decolonization: Politics, Nationalism and the Police, 1917–65* (Manchester, 1992)

Andrews, C. S., *Dublin Made Me* (Dublin, 2001)

Anonymous, *Tales of the RIC* (London, 1921)

Augusteijn, Joost, *From Public Defiance to Guerrilla Warfare: Experiences of Ordinary Volunteers in the Irish War of Independence 1916–21* (Dublin, 1996)

—, *The Irish Revolution 1913–23* (New York, 2002)

—, *The Memoirs of John M. Regan, a Catholic officer in the RIC and RUC, 1909–48* (Dublin, 2007)

Ball, Stephen, *A Policeman's Ireland: Recollections of Samuel Waters, RIC* (Cork, 1999)

Barry, Tom, *Guerrilla Days in Ireland* (Dublin, 1949)

Bartlett, Thomas and Jeffrey, Keith, *A Military History of Ireland* (Cambridge, 1996)

Béaslaí, Piaras, *Michael Collins and the Making of a New Ireland* (London, 1926)

Bennett, Richard, *The Black and Tans* (New York, 1959)

Blackstock, Allan, *An Ascendancy Army: The Irish Yeomanry, 1796–1834* (Dublin, 1998)

Borgonovo, John, *Spies, Informers and the Anti-Sinn Féin Society: The Intelligence War in Cork City, 1920–21* (Dublin, 2007)

Boyce, D. George and O'Day, Alan (eds), *The Making of Modern Irish History, Revisionism and the Revisionist Controversy* (Oxford, 1996)

Brady, Conor, *Guardians of the Peace* (Dublin, 1974)

Breathnach, Séamus, *The Irish Police* (Dublin, 1974)

Breen, Dan, *My Fight for Irish Freedom* (Dublin, 1924)

Brewer, John, *The Royal Irish Constabulary: An Oral History* (Belfast, 1990)

Broeker, Galen, *Rural Disorder and Police Reform in Ireland, 1812–36* (London 1970)

Campbell, Fergus, *Politics in the West of Ireland, 1891–1921* (Oxford, 2005)

Coleman, Marie, *County Longford and the Irish Revolution, 1910–23* (Dublin, 2003)

Coogan, Tim Pat, *De Valera: Long Fellow, Long Shadow* (London, 1993)

Cornewall Lewis, George, *On Local Disturbances in Ireland: And on the Irish Church Question* (London, 1836)

Costello, Con, *A Most Delightful Station* (Dublin, 1999)

Costello, Francis, *The Irish Revolution and its Aftermath, 1916–23: Years of Revolt* (Dublin, 2003)

Crozier, Brigadier General Frank, *Impressions and Collections* (London, 1930)

—, *Ireland for Ever* (London, 1932)

Curtis, Robert, *The History of the Royal Irish Constabulary* (London, 1869)

Duff, Douglas V., *Sword for Hire: The Saga of a Modern Free-Companion* (London, 1934)

Dwyer, T. Ryle, *Tans, Terror and Troubles* (Cork, 2001)

Ellis, Stephen, *Tudor Ireland: Crown, Community and the Conflict of Cultures, 1470–1603* (London, 1985)

English, Richard, *Ernie O'Malley: IRA Intellectual* (London, 1999)

English, Richard, *Irish Freedom: The History of Nationalism in Ireland* (London, 2006)

Farry, Michael, *The Aftermath of Revolution, Sligo 1921–3* (Dublin, 2000)

Fennell, Thomas, *The Royal Irish Constabulary* (Dublin, 2003)

Fitzpatrick, David, *Politics and Irish Life, 1913–21: Provincial Experiences of War and Revolution* (Cork, 1977) and *The Two Irelands, 1912–39* (Oxford, 1998)

Foy, Michael T., *Michael Collins's Intelligence War: The Struggle Between the British And the IRA, 1919–21* (Gloucester, 2006)

Garvin, Tom, *Nationalist Revolutionaries in Ireland, 1858–1928* (Dublin, 1986)

Gash, Norman, *Peel: A Condensed Version of Mr Secretary Peel (1961) and Sir Robert Peel (1972)* (Dublin, 1976)

Gilbert, Martin, *Winston Churchill: World in Torment, Vol. IV, 1916–22* (London, 1975)

Griffith, Kenneth and O'Grady, Timothy, *Curious Journey: An Oral History of Ireland's Unfinished Revolution* (London, 1998)

Grob-Fitzgibbon, Benjamin, *Turning Points of the Irish Revolution: The British Government, Intelligence and the Cost of Indifference, 1912–21* (New York, 2007)

Gurney, Russell, *History of the Northamptonshire Regiment, 1742–1934* (Aldershot, 1935)

Gwynn, Denis, *De Valera* (London, 1933)

Handcock, W. D. and Young, G. M., *English Historical Documents, 1874–1914, Vol. 10.* (London, 1996)

Hart, Peter, *The IRA and its Enemies: Violence and Community in Cork, 1916–23* (Oxford, 1999)

—, *British Intelligence in Ireland, 1920–21: The Final Reports* (Cork, 2002)

—, *The IRA at War, 1916–23* (Oxford, 2003)

—, *Mick: The Real Michael Collins* (London, 2005)

Hawkins, Richard, 'Dublin Castle and the Royal Irish Constabulary', in Williams, Desmond T. (ed.), *The Irish Struggle, 1916–26* (London, 1966)

Herlihy, James, *The Royal Irish Constabulary: A Short History and Genealogical Guide* (Dublin, 1997)

—, *Royal Irish Constabulary Officers: A Biographical Dictionary and Genealogical Guide, 1816–1922* (Dublin, 2005)

Holt, Edgar, *Protest in Arms: The Irish Troubles, 1916–23* (New York, 1960)

Hopkinson, Michael, *The Irish War of Independence* (Dublin, 2002)

—, *The Last Days of Dublin Castle: The Diaries of Mark Sturgis* (Dublin, 1999)

—, *Green Against Green: The Irish Civil War* (London, 2004)

Howe, Stephen, *Ireland and Empire: Colonial Legacies in Irish History and Culture* (Oxford, 2000)

Hurd, Douglas, *Sir Robert Peel: A Biography* (London, 2007)

Jeffrey, Keith, *The British Army and Crisis of Empire, 1918–22* (Manchester, 1984)

Joy, Sinéad, *The IRA in Kerry, 1916–21* (Cork, 2005)

Kee, Robert, *The Green Flag: A History of Irish Nationalism* (London, 1972)

Kenny, Kevin (ed.), *Ireland and British Empire: Oxford History of the British Empire Companion Series* (Oxford, 2004)

Leeson, D. M., *The Black and Tans: British Police and Auxiliaries in the Irish War of Independence* (Oxford, 2011)
Loft, Martin, *Lieutenant Harry Loft and the 64th Regiment of Foot* (Stafford, 2003)
Lyons, F. S. L., *Ireland since the Famine* (London, 1971)
Macardle, Dorothy, *The Irish Republic: A Documented Chronicle of the Anglo-Irish Conflict and the Partitioning of Ireland, with a Detailed Account of the Period, 1916–23* (Dublin, 1951)
McGarry, Fearghal, *Eoin O'Duffy: A Self-Made Hero* (Oxford, 2005)
MacNevin, Thomas, *The Speeches of Richard Lalor Sheil* (Dublin, 1845)
Macready, General Sir Nevil, *Annals of an Active Life,* Volumes I and II (London, 1924)
Malcolm, Elizabeth, *The Irish Policeman, 1822–1922: A Life* (Dublin, 2006)
May, Trevor, *Military Barracks* (Buckinghamshire, 2002)
Murphy Gerard, *The Year of Disappearances: Political Killings in Cork 1921–22* (Dublin, 2010)
Murray, Patrick, *Oracles of God: The Roman Catholic and Irish politics,* 1922–37 (Dublin, 2000)
Mulcahy, Risteárd, *My Father, the General: Richard Mulcahy and the Military History of the Revolution* (Dublin, 2009)
Nelligan, David, *The Spy in the Castle* (London, 1968)
Nelson, Ivan F., *The Irish Militia, 1793–1802* (Dublin, 2007)
Mitchell, Arthur, *Revolutionary Government in Ireland: Dáil Éireann, 1919–22* (Dublin, 1995)
O'Callaghan, John, *Revolutionary Limerick: The Republican Campaign for Independence in Limerick, 1913–21* (Dublin, 2010)
O'Donnell, Stephen, *The RIC and the Black and Tans in County Louth, 1919–22* (Drogheda, 2004)
O'Haicead, Padraig, *Keep Their Names Ever Green* (Nenagh, 2003)
O'Hegarty, P. S., *A History of Ireland under the Union, 1801–1922* (London, 1952)
O'Malley, Ernie, *On Another Man's Wound* (Dublin, 1936)
—, *The Singing Flame* (Dublin, 1978)
—, *Raids and Rallies* (Dublin, 1982)
O'Sullivan, Donal, *The Irish Constabularies, 1822–1922: A Century of Policing in Ireland* (Kerry, 1999)

Oxford Companion to Irish History (New York, 2011)
Palmer, Stanley, *Police and Protest in England and Ireland 1780–1850* (Cambridge, 1988)
Paul-Dubois, Louis, *Contemporary Ireland* (Dublin, 1908)
Philips, W. Allison, *The Revolution in Ireland, 1906–23* (London, 1926)
Rumpf, E. and Hepburn, A. C., *Nationalism and Socialism in Twentieth-Century Ireland* (Liverpool, 1977)
Ryan, Brendan, *Policing in West Offaly, 1814–1922* (Tullamore, 2009)
Ryan, Desmond, *Seán Treacy and the Third Tipperary Brigade* (Tralee, 1945)
Ryan, Meda, *Tom Barry: IRA Freedom Fighter* (Dublin, 2003)
Shea, Patrick, *Voices and the Sounds of Drums: An Irish Autobiography* (Belfast, 1981)
Townshend, Charles, *The British Campaign in Ireland, 1919–21: The Development of Political and Military Policies* (Oxford, 1975)
Townshend, Charles, *Political Violence in Ireland: Government and Resistance since 1848* (Oxford, 1983)
Walsh, Maurice, *The News from Ireland: Foreign Correspondents and the Irish Revolution* (London, 2008)
Whelan, Bernadette, *American Government in Ireland, 1790–1913: A History of the US Consular Service* (Manchester, 2010)
White, Terence de Vere, *Kevin O'Higgins* (Dublin, 1966)

Unpublished Theses

Bridgeman, Ian, 'Policing Rural Ireland: A study of the Origins, Development and Role of the Irish Constabulary, and its Impact on Crime Prevention and Detection in the Nineteenth Century' (PhD thesis, Open University, 1993)
Grayson, Natasha, 'The Quality Of Nationalism in Counties Cavan, Louth and Meath during the Irish Revolution' (PhD thesis, Keele, 2007)
Leeson, David, 'The Black and Tans: British Police in the First Irish War, 1920–21' (PhD thesis, McMaster University, 2003)

Journals

Carden, Arthur, 'Templemore Houses and Castles, Drawings by Robert Smith', *Tipperary Historical Journal* (2002)

Fedorowich, Kent, 'The Problems of Disbandment: The Royal Irish Constabulary and Imperial Migration, 1919–29', *Irish Historical Studies*, Vol. XXX, no. 117, May (1996)

Gaynor, Sean, 'With Tipperary No. 1 Brigade in North Tipperary 1917–21, Part 1', *Tipperary Historical Journal* (1993)

Ghotzardis, Evi, 'Revisionist Historians and the Modern Irish State: The Conflict between the Advisory Committee and the Bureau of Military History, 1947–66', *Irish Historical Studies*, Vol. XXXV May (2006)

Kinnane, Paddy, 'My Part in the War of Independence, Part II', *Tipperary Historical Journal* (1996)

Lowe, W. J., 'The Constabulary Agitation of 1882', *Irish Historical Studies*, xxx1, no. 121 (May, 1998)

—, 'The War against the RIC', *Eire-Ireland: Journal of Irish Studies* (Fall–Winter, 2002)

—, 'Who Were the Black and Tans?' in *History Ireland* (Autumn, 2004)

— and E. L. Malcolm, 'The Domestication of the Royal Irish Constabulary', *Irish Economic and Social History*, Vol. XIX (1992)

O'Callaghan, Margaret, 'New Ways of Looking at the State Apparatus and the State Archive in Nineteenth-Century Ireland', *Proceedings of the Royal Irish Academy*, Vol. 104C, No. 2 (2004)

Online Sources

Biography of Seamus Bourke TD, Official Website of the Oireachtas (www.oireachtas.ie) (Accessed 11 April 2012)

Hansard House of Lords Debate on the Soloheadbeg Ambush, 20 March 1919 (http://hansard.millbanksystems.com/lords/1919/mar/20/the-tragedy-at soloheadbeg#S5LV0033P0_19190320_HOL_166) (Accessed 22 November 2011).

McPherson, James, 'Revisionist Historians' in *Perspectives: The Journal of the American Historical Association,* September 2003 (www.historians.org/perspectives/issues/2003/0309/0309pre1.cfm) (Accessed 1 September 2008)

Index